Science
Made Simple

•••••••••••••••••••••••••••••••

Grade 3

Written by Q. L. Pearce
Illustrated by Sherry Neidigh

FS-23213 Science Made Simple Grade 3
All rights reserved–Printed in the U.S.A.
Copyright © 1997 Frank Schaffer Publications
23740 Hawthorne Blvd.
Torrance, CA 90505

Introduction

Because of their natural curiosity, children are born scientists. This book presents a variety of experiments, discovery activities, demonstrations, and suggestions for classroom

What is a living thing?

Does air have weight?

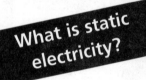

What is static electricity?

Why does the moon seem to change shape?

presentations that will get students involved in the processes of science and so help nurture that curiosity.

Science Made Simple Grade 3 can be used alone or as an integral part of any science program. The book is organized into three sections, each focusing on a major discipline: Life Science, Physical Science, and Earth Science. Flexible enough to complement any curriculum, it incorporates a variety of science skills.

The experiments, discovery activities, and science fair suggestions included are designed to be safe and simple, and most require materials that are inexpensive and readily available. When guiding students through activities, ask plenty of open-ended questions to promote creativity and divergent thinking. Encourage students to look for alternative answers, work in groups, and share information. In particular, make it clear to students that there are no dumb questions and no wasted results. Even a disproven hypothesis provides information that may be useful in the next experiment.

Science is naturally fun for students as long as you remain flexible. In the early stages of science education, gaining an understanding of the process is the most important goal. With that in mind, assure students that there are no wrong answers when developing a hypothesis. Even if their guesses prove to be incorrect, they can still learn from the results. Science is a creative process so give students plenty of time to ask questions, work together in groups, share information, and develop alternative approaches to each problem. Be sure to have plenty of workspace and equipment available so that everyone can participate. Science safety for all involved in the classroom or during home experiments is simple if students stick to a few basic rules:

*Always read through or plan the experiment before beginning.

*If necessary, cover work surfaces with newspaper.

*Know your tools and ingredients.

*Never put an unknown material in your mouth or eyes.

*If an experiment calls for warm or hot water, wear protective gloves and an apron.

*Know when to ask for help.

*Clean work areas when finished.

*Wash hands after experiments.

*Respect the property of others.

*Do no harm to living things.

It is hoped that as you implement the ideas in this book, your students will become better observers, questioners, and problem-solvers. It is also hoped that as your students conduct various investigations, they will enjoy science as a fun, rewarding, and meaningful part of their school experience.

Life Science

No matter where you travel on Earth, from the deepest ocean to the highest mountain, from the equator to the poles, you will find living things. Life science introduces your students to the amazing world of plants and animals, and readies them to see their own place in the web of life.

CONCEPTS

In the following section, your students will discover the following concepts:

- *Living things have basic needs and need certain things to grow.*

- *Plants are essential living things.*

- *Plants are classified into two groups—plants that make seeds and plants that do not make seeds.*

- *Animals share certain characteristics.*

- *Animals are classified into two groups—those with backbones and those without backbones.*

LIFE SCIENCE RESOURCES

Books for Students

Projects for a Healthy Planet by Shar Levine and Allison Grafton (John Wiley & Sons, 1992). This is a collection of easy-to-do, low-cost activities that help students learn more about pollution, recycling, and environmentally friendly products.

The Big Green Book by Fred Pearce (Kingfisher Books, 1991). In an extremely simple approach, this book examines many of the environmental problems that face the world today, including overpopulation, pollution, and deforestation.

Biology for Every Kid by Janice VanCleave (John Wiley & Sons, 1990). This book has 101 simple experiments about plants, animals, and the human body.

Web Sites

Ranger Rick home page (http://www.nwf.org/nwf) Click on "For Kids!" Then click on Ranger Rick.

The Wonders of the Seas (http://wilmot.unh.edu/~krasuski/)

Rainforest Action Network (http://www.ran.org/ran) Click on Kids' Corner.

Organizations

National Audubon Society, 950 Third Avenue, New York, NY 10022

The Wilderness Society, 1400 Eye Street NW, Washington, D.C. 20005

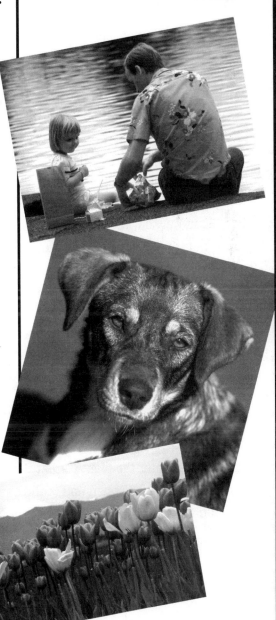

Living and Nonliving Things

All living things have basic needs. Living things need certain things to grow. For example, living things need food, water, and gases to breathe. As you give your class opportunities to compare nonliving things to living things, your students will begin to identify the characteristics that all living things share.

WHAT IS A LIVING THING?

Class Activity

Materials: a copy of page 3 for each student; samples of living and nonliving things (Use toys or pictures from magazines when the real thing is impractical. You might include a variety of plants, animals (choose some fun ones like a natural sponge or a starfish), rocks, a doll, an ice cube, and something made from an animal product, such as a leather glove.)

What to Do: Write these five characteristics of living things on the board:

> *Living things take in nutrients (food).*
> *Living things give off wastes.*
> *Living things grow.*
> *Living things reproduce.*
> *Living things respond to their environment.*

Have students read the cartoon on page 3. Then lead them in a discussion about it. Explain that, in a way, the crystal grows. However, it doesn't fulfill the other requirements and is not alive. Point out that the car may take in fuel and give off exhaust fumes, but it isn't alive. Discuss how plants and animals do meet the criteria. Display the items you have assembled and ask students to determine which are living and which are not.

LET'S EXPERIMENT: WATER WASTE

Class Experiment

This experiment will show one way that plants eliminate waste.

Materials: copies of pages 4–5 for each student or group; one leafy, potted plant such as a pothos or geranium; one small plastic bag; one twist tie (tape or string will also work); water; sunny window

What to Do: Water the plant so that the soil is very moist. Have a student place the plastic bag over several leaves and secure the open end of the bag to the stem with a twist tie. Place the plant in a sunny window. Have the students check the experiment every 30 minutes.

Results: Drops of water will eventually form inside the bag. Excess water vapor escapes from the leaves through tiny openings called stomata. Oxygen, a by-product of photosynthesis, also exits through the stomata.

FS-23213 Science Made Simple ▪ © Frank Schaffer Publications, Inc.

Living or Nonliving

Let's Experiment: Water Waste

Problem:
Is a plant a living thing?

What Do I Know?
Living things eliminate waste.

Question:
Do plants eliminate waste?

Materials:
leafy, potted plant
plastic bag with twist tie
water
sunny window

Predict:
Through their leaves and roots, plants take in sunlight, air, water, and nutrients. If plants give off waste, it might be eliminated through the leaves. What do you think you will find out if you cover some of the leaves with plastic? Write your prediction on your record sheet.

What to Do:
1. Water the plant so that the soil is damp.

2. Slip the plastic bag over several leaves, then close the open end with a twist tie.

3. Place the plant in a sunny window.

Collecting and Analyzing Information:
Check your experiment three times, 30 minutes apart. On your record sheet, write down what you see.

Conclusion:
Do my results help to show that a plant is a living thing? How? Write your answers on your record sheet.

FS-23213 Science Made Simple ▪ © Frank Schaffer Publications, Inc.

Plants Where I Live

Problem:
Is a plant a living thing?

What Do I Know?
Living things eliminate waste.

Question:
Do plants eliminate waste?

Predict:
What do you think you will find out if you cover some of the leaves with

plastic? _____

_____

Collecting and Analyzing Information:

First check: Time _____ What I saw_____

_____

Second check: Time _____ What I saw_____

_____

Third check: Time _____ What I saw_____

_____

Conclusion:
Does my experiment help to show that a plant is a living thing? _____

How?_____

_____

Think About It:
Plants give off water vapor through their leaves. They also give off oxygen
through their leaves. Can you think of an experiment that could show this?

_____

_____

WHY CLASSIFY?

Explain to your students that scientists have organized all living things into five large groups, called kingdoms, to make them easier to study. You will focus on two kingdoms: plant and animal. Each kingdom is divided into smaller and smaller groups organized by the characteristics the members have in common. In this activity, students will discover how classification works by classifying nonliving items.

Materials: 3" x 5" cards labeled *Tools*, *Toys*, and *Clothes*; 8 to 10 display items that will fit into these categories (Use pictures from magazines if the real object is impractical. Be sure to include objects that can be categorized in different ways. A plastic hammer, for example, might be a tool, but it isn't good for hammering a nail. It is more likely a toy. Explain that sometimes even scientists disagree when categorizing living things. Have the students work together to decide in which category each display item belongs.)

As a follow-up activity, have students classify plants and animals into two kingdoms by completing *Which Kingdom?* (page 7).

Answers: Plant Kingdom—Geranium, Lily, Cactus, Fern, Pine Tree, Rose

Animal Kingdom—Shark, Owl, Dog, Horse, Trout, Hummingbird

SPOTLIGHT ON SCIENTISTS

Give students copies of *Spotlight on Scientists* (page 8). Ask them to read the story about Carolus Linnaeus and then answer the questions. Explain that when Carolus Linnaeus was a young boy, his father wanted him to study for the ministry, but he was so interested in plants that his friends convinced his parents to send him to medical school. Have your students each write down what they would like to study. Then have the students go home and ask their parents what they would like them to study. Have the class share their results.

Answers: (1) Sweden; (2) a botanist; (3) Latin; (4) sometimes the common names for plants and animals get mixed up; (5) into groups according to shared characteristics

Language Arts Link/ Art Smart

The plants listed below have names that make them sound like animals. Write the names on the board. Explain that these are the names of real plants. Then ask students to draw imaginative pictures of what the plants might look like. Let students be creative and have fun with this one!

Dogwood

Catnip

Snake Plant

Cowslip

Elephant's-ear Plant

Which Kingdom?

There are millions of different kinds of living things on Earth. To make them easier to study, scientists put living things into groups. The things in each group are alike in certain ways. The biggest groups are called *kingdoms*.

List the plants and animals below in the correct kingdom.

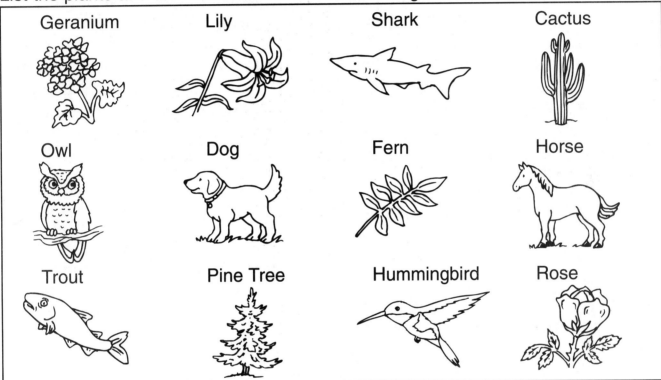

Geranium   Lily   Shark   Cactus

Owl   Dog   Fern   Horse

Trout   Pine Tree   Hummingbird   Rose

Plant Kingdom		Animal Kingdom	
_____	_____	_____	_____
_____	_____	_____	_____
_____	_____	_____	_____

In what ways are these members of the plant kingdom alike?

_____

In what ways are these members of the animal kingdom alike?

_____

Spotlight on Scientists

Carolus Linnaeus was born in 1707. He was a Swedish doctor and botanist (someone who studies plants). He made up a system of scientific names for living things. Each living thing was given two Latin names. That made it easier for everyone because sometimes the common names for plants and animals could get mixed up. For example, the bird known as a robin in England is different from the bird known as a robin in the United States. By using the Latin names, scientists always knew they were talking about the same thing.

Under Linnaeus' system, the first name stands for the genus (or race), and the second name stands for the species (or kind). The animals or plants in a group are like each other in important ways. For example, wolves and dogs both belong to the genus *Canis*. Later on, other scientists came up with a more complete system. Now all living things are organized into groups according to shared characteristics.

Answer the following questions.

1. What country was Carolus Linnaeus from? _____

2. What do you call someone who studies plants? _____

3. Living things are given two names in what language? _____

4. Why is it important to have scientific names for plants and animals? _____

_____

_____

5. How are living things organized today? _____

_____

_____

_____

FS-23213 Science Made Simple ▪ © Frank Schaffer Publications, Inc.

Plant Kingdom

Plants are essential to other living things. They produce the oxygen we breathe as well as provide important products for us. By introducing your students to the fascinating world of plants, they will discover how vital plants are to human life.

THE IMPORTANCE OF PLANTS

Class Activity ....

Your students are probably familiar with a wide variety of plants, but they might not have thought about how valuable plants are to other living things. Lead the class in a discussion of the importance of plants. Begin by asking your students what they had for breakfast. If it was cereal or toast with jam, the connection is direct. If they had eggs, bacon, or milk, the animals those things come from were plant-eaters, so the connection is indirect. Here are some other important uses of plants:

Clothing: Cotton and linen are examples of cloth made from plants. Some plants, such as yarrow and geranium, can be used to produce dyes. Grasses and reeds can be woven into purses and hats.

Shelter and Furnishings: Look around the classroom and point out things made of wood. Wood is used in the construction of buildings and furniture. Don't forget to mention that pencils and paper are made from plant products. Products made of rubber might also be found in the classroom.

Your Health: Plants take in carbon dioxide and release oxygen as a by-product of photosynthesis. For every deep breath we take, we can thank a plant. Also, many important medicines and health products come from plants.

Look Outside: Explain that plant roots hold soil in place and ground covering plants also keep soil from washing or blowing away. Trees and bushes provide homes and shelter for animals.

As a homework assignment, ask students to write down every time they use plants or plant materials in a 24-hour period.

SCIENCE FAIR FUN

Class Activity ......

Let your students do research to find out what the different plant groups are and what the characteristics of each group are. Students can make a plant classification display by taping two pieces of 2' x 3' posterboard together. On one piece, the students write out the characteristics that determine a living thing as a plant. On the other piece, they list the major plant groups and their characteristics and then glue a sample or drawing of the type of plant onto the board.

WHAT'S THE DIFFERENCE?

This activity will show the most obvious differences between plants and animals.

You will need a supply of "plant" stickers. These can be as simple as green dots. Prepare a display with pictures of a wide variety of plants and animals. Try to include a picture of a lacy-looking coral, a jellyfish, a walking stick insect, or any other creature that might be mistaken for a plant. If possible, also include a picture of an insect-eating plant such as a sundew or pitcher plant.

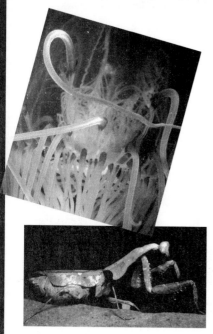

Explain to students that one of the main differences between plants and animals is that most plants don't have to find and eat food. They make their own food from sunlight, air, and water. Another difference is that animals move about freely from place to place during all or at least some part of their lives. Once your students understand these differences, ask them to identify the plants in the display. Place a sticker on each. If a student chooses the coral, explain that it is a colony of small creatures that filter-feed seawater.

When the activity is complete, explain that plants are basically divided into two groups—plants that make seeds and plants that do not make seeds. Plants that make seeds are flowering plants and conifers. Plants that do not make seeds are ferns, club mosses, mosses, and liverworts. Explain that you will be focusing on the largest group—the flowering plants. Then have students complete *A Flowering Plant* (page 11).

LET'S EXPERIMENT: LIVING ON LIGHT

This experiment will show whether or not plants need sunlight in order to thrive.

Materials: copies of pages 12–13 for each student or group; two potted plants of the same type, such as geraniums or pothos; one cardboard box large enough to cover a plant

What to Do: Start this experiment on a Monday. Number the plants *1* and *2*. Place plant number one in a sunny location. Place the cardboard box over plant number two so it doesn't get light. Care for the plants in the same manner, giving each adequate water. Check the health of both plants three times over the course of the week. At the end of the experiment, put plant number two in the sunny window to see if its condition will change.

Results: In the first experiment, the plant that has been deprived of light will become pale and sickly. Green plants need sunlight in order to produce their food. Have the students observe how long it takes for the plant to return to health once it gets light.

Something More: Ask students to design an experiment to show whether or not plants need air or water.

FS-23213 Science Made Simple ▪ © Frank Schaffer Publications, Inc.

A Flowering Plant

There are more than 350,000 kinds of plants on Earth! Most are flowering plants that produce seeds. Flowering plants come in all shapes and sizes, but they are made up of the same basic parts.

Not all seed-bearing plants have flowers. Trees such as pine and fir produce their seeds on cones. Have you ever seen a pine cone? Some plants don't have seeds at all. Ferns and mosses produce little parts called spores that can grow into new plants.

Read the description of the plant parts below. Then label the parts in the drawing with the correct names.

Leaves are food factories. Sunlight, air, and water are combined there to make a plant's food. Leaves also take in air and release oxygen and water vapor.

Roots anchor a plant into the soil or on the branch where it is growing. Roots take in water and dissolved minerals that a plant needs to help make its food.

The **stem** supports a plant. Water and important nutrients are carried from the roots, through the stem, to the rest of the plant.

Flowers are the reproductive parts of a plant. They are made up of different parts that help the plant to produce seeds. Some flowers are pretty and colorful.

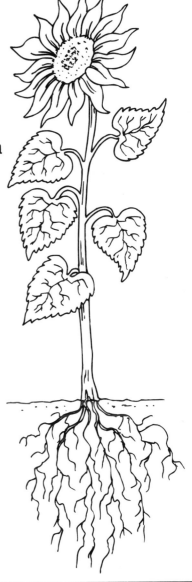

Let's Experiment: Living on Light

Problem:
What do green plants need to be healthy?

What Do I Know?
Plants make their own food.

Question:
Do plants need sunlight to help them make their food?

Materials:
two leafy, potted plants
a cardboard box (or space on a closet shelf)
felt-tip marker
water
sunny window

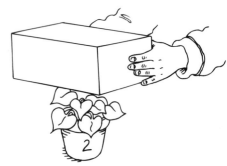

Predict:
Like all living things, plants need food. Most green plants spend at least part of each day in sunlight. Does sunlight help plants to make food that keeps them healthy? What do you think you will find out if you keep a green plant in darkness? Write your prediction on your record sheet.

What to Do:
1. Label one plant #1 and the other #2.
2. Place plant #1 in a protected, sunny spot.
3. Place plant #2 under the cardboard box so that it gets no sunlight.
4. Be sure the soil in each plant stays slightly moist throughout the experiment.

Collecting and Analyzing Information:
Check each plant three times in five days. On your record sheet, write down what you see.

Conclusion:
Do my results help to show that a plant needs sunlight? How? Write your answers on your record sheet.

FS-23213 Science Made Simple ▪ © Frank Schaffer Publications, Inc.

Let's Experiment: Living on Light

Problem:
What do green plants need to be healthy?

What Do I Know?
Plants make their own food.

Question:
Do plants need sunlight to help them make their food?

Predict:
What do you think will happen if you keep a green plant in darkness?

_____

_____

Collecting and Analyzing Information:

First check: Day and Time_____

What I saw_____

Second check: Day and Time_____

What I saw_____

Final check: Day and Time_____

What I saw_____

Conclusion:
Does my experiment help to show that plants need sunlight? How?

_____

_____

Fun Fact:
Plants have a special material in their leaves called chlorophyll (KLOR-o-fil) that "soaks" in light. Sunlight is made up of different colors of light, and chlorophyll soaks up red and blue light, but not much green. Most green light is bounced back to your eye, and that is why the plants look green.

THE ROOT OF THE MATTER

Fast-growing bean plants are an excellent way to demonstrate root growth.

Materials: six dried lima beans; large glass jar; blotting paper; paper towels; water; small towel

What to Do: Soak the beans in water overnight. The following morning, line the inside of the jar with blotting paper. Stuff paper towels in the center and fill the jar with water. After about five minutes, drain the jar. Slip the beans between the glass and the blotting paper about halfway down the side of the jar. Cover the jar with a small towel and check it after two or three days. You might have to spray the blotting paper with water to keep it moist. Once the sprouting has started, remove the towel and your display is ready.

Students can keep track of the little plants' progress by measuring stem and root growth. Once the plants have started, you can turn the jar on its side for a couple of days to show that the roots always grow down. This response to gravity is called geotropism.

ROOTS AND STEMS

There are many different kinds of root systems. Basically, they can be broken into two main types, fibrous roots, and taproots. Bring an example of each for display in class. Taproots are main, central roots. You might choose a carrot as an example of a taproot. Fibrous roots branch out in many directions. Grasses have fibrous roots. Many types of houseplants have fibrous roots as well, and can be lifted from their pots to expose the roots without harming the plant.

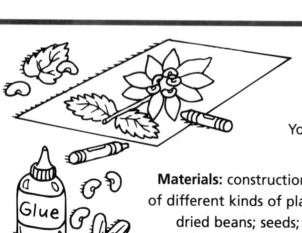

Art Project

Art **S**mart: **P**retty **P**lants

Your students will probably enjoy using a potpourri of materials to make their own plant collages.

Materials: construction paper; glue; scissors; crayons; magazine pictures of different kinds of plants; yarn; pipe cleaners; scraps of fabric; buttons; dried beans; seeds; dried leaves; tissue paper; aluminum foil; sequins

What to Do: Have students choose a picture and then make their own collage version of the plant by gluing the materials you have provided to construction paper. For example, they could make pipe cleaner stems, dried leaves, and tissue-paper flowers with sequins in the center.

LANGUAGE LINK

Roots anchor a plant in place and are usually unseen underground. Write these sentences on the board and ask students to explain why the word *root* is used to express each idea.

Tom couldn't hit a baseball. The root of the problem was in how he held his bat.

Bill and his family planned to move to a new town and put down their roots.

Ashley rooted around in her backpack for a pencil.

LET'S EXPERIMENT: FROM HERE TO THERE
Class Experiment

Water and nutrients travel from the roots of a plant, up the stem, to all parts of the plant. This experiment will show that something entering the plant at the base will travel to the tips of the flowers.

Materials: copies of pages 16–17 for each student or group; a fresh white carnation; a sharp knife; red and blue food coloring; water; two small glass jars

What to Do: Have students prepare the jars by filling each one about two inches full with water and adding enough food coloring to darken the water. Put red food coloring in one jar and blue in the other.

Cut the stem of the carnation carefully in half. Make the cut just long enough so that a student can place one side in the red jar and one in the blue jar. Place the jars in a warm spot for about an hour, then check.

Results: The tips of the carnation petals should be slightly colored. The food coloring in the water has been drawn up the stem and distributed throughout the plant. The side of the flower in the blue coloring will be tinted blue. The side of the flower in the red coloring will be tinted red.

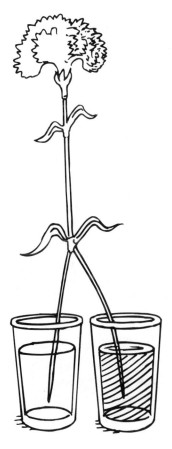

Let's Experiment: From Here to There

Problem:
How do nutrients in the soil get into a plant?

What Do I Know?
Plant roots absorb water from the soil.

Question:
Will nutrients in the water reach all of the plant?

Materials:
two glass jars
red and blue food coloring
a fresh white carnation with a split stem
water

Predict:
Plants use water and carbon dioxide from the air in their food-making process. They also need certain minerals from the soil to thrive. Do you think that mixing those minerals with water will help them to travel throughout the plant? Write your prediction on your record sheet.

What to Do:
1. Fill one jar with two inches of water and enough red food coloring to darken the water.

2. Fill the other jar with the same amount of water and blue food coloring.

3. Place one side of the carnation stem in jar #1 and the other in jar #2.

4. Set the experiment aside and do not disturb it.

Collecting and Analyzing Information:
Check the flower after 30 minutes and again after one hour. On your record sheet, write down what you see.

Conclusion:
Does my experiment help to show that nutrients that are dissolved in water will reach all parts of a plant? How? Write your answers on your record sheet.

FS-23213 Science Made Simple ▪ © Frank Schaffer Publications, Inc.

Let's Experiment: From Here to There

Problem:
How do nutrients in the soil get into a plant?

What Do I Know?
Plant roots absorb water from the soil.

Question:
Will nutrients in the water reach all of the plant?

Predict:
Plants need certain minerals from the soil to thrive. Do you think that mixing those minerals with water will help them to travel throughout the plant?

_____

_____

Collecting and Analyzing Information:

First check: Time _____ What I saw _____

_____

Final check: Time _____ What I saw _____

_____

Conclusion:
Does my experiment help to show that nutrients that are dissolved in water will reach all parts of a plant? How?

_____

_____

Think About It:
If a plant thrives when it is given nutrient-rich water, what will happen to it

if it is given polluted water? _____

Do you think that pollutants might reach the parts of the plant that animals

and people eat? _____

INSIDE A SEED

········· Class Activity ·····

This demonstration, which uses lima beans, can be accomplished with no cutting, so provide each student with a seed of his or her own. Packets can be purchased inexpensively at a garden supply store.

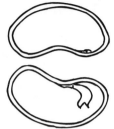

Soak the beans for 24 hours ahead of time. Have the students remove the outer skin if there is any. Then have them gently pry apart the two halves along the natural opening. There should be a very tiny plant at one end called the embryo. Ask students to describe the embryo. Ask what they think the rest of the seed is for (food for the new plant), why the seed is hard (protection), and what will happen when the seed is planted.

To extend the activity, have students bring in other examples of seeds. Ask students to think of examples of types of seeds we eat, such as sesame, sunflower, etc.

ADOPT-A-TREE

···· Class Activity ····

Choose a tree in the schoolyard or in a local park that is accessible to all students, and adopt it as your class tree. Make it a class project to find out everything possible about the tree. For example: *What kind of tree is it? What animals are found on it? Does it have seasonal changes? Is the bark rough? Are the stems smooth or sticky? Does it have thorns? How big is it? How do the leaves feel? Are the shapes and textures different on different parts of the plant? Does it have flowers? If so, how do* *they smell?* If possible, have students grow seedlings from the tree.

SURPRISE GARDEN

······ Class Experiment ····

Ask each student to write his or her name on a paper cup and then fill the cup with soil from his or her yard, a vacant lot, or a park. Have students bring their cups to class. Place the cups in a warm, sunny spot and water them so that the soil remains slightly moist. Observe over a week or two to see if anything grows.

Art Project

Art Smart: Making a Plant Press

Dried leaves and flowers can be used in many art projects. You don't need special equipment, just newspaper for lining and a large book that will enable you to press leaves and small flowers between the pages (changing the newspaper every so often until the object is dry). For bigger jobs, a classroom press is not difficult to make.

Materials: two 8½" x 11" pieces of plywood with holes drilled at each corner; four bolts with wing nuts to fit in the holes; blotting paper cut to fit press; corrugated cardboard cut to fit press; newspaper cut to fit press

What to Do: Make a stack with one piece of plywood, then corrugated cardboard, blotting paper, and newspaper. Place the leaves or flowers on the newspaper in any arrangement. Top with another piece of newspaper, blotting paper, corrugated cardboard, and then the second piece of plywood. Slip the bolts through the holes at the corners of the two pieces of plywood and turn the wing nuts until they are finger tight. Leave the press in a warm, dry place. Depending on what you are drying, the process will take two to four weeks.

Animal Kingdom

All animals share certain characteristics: they breathe, take in food, and reproduce. Let your students discover more about the amazing world of animals with the following activities.

THE WORLD OF ANIMALS
Class Activity

On the board, list different types of pets, including dogs, cats, fish, birds, turtles, snakes, mice, and hamsters. Call out each category and ask students who have that type of pet to raise their hands. Explain that one thing we depend on animals for is companionship. Next, ask students to think of other things that we depend on animals for. Write their answers on the board. (Examples: food; clothing such as wool and leather; transportation) Students might not consider the value of insects, so point out that certain insects pollinate plants, while others eat dead plants and animals, thereby eliminating waste.

WHAT IS A VERTEBRATE?
Group Activity

Explain to students that the animal kingdom is basically divided into two groups—those with backbones (vertebrates) and those without (invertebrates). Have them reach back and feel their own backbones. Then ask them what they think they are for. Point out that the backbone gives support and protects the spine.

Explain to your class that there are different groups of vertebrates. There are mammals, birds, reptiles, amphibians, and fish. Let your class know that each group shares certain characteristics that the other groups do not. Divide your class into five teams, and assign an animal group to each team. Have the students work together to learn interesting facts about their groups, then have each team present the facts to the rest of the class.

Students can complete *Amazing Animals* (page 20) as a follow-up activity.

Answers: newt (amphibian); turtle (reptile); shark (fish); ostrich (bird); frog (amphibian); crocodile (reptile); human (mammal); monkey (mammal); trout (fish); eagle (bird)

WHAT IS AN INVERTEBRATE?
Class Activity

Explain to your class that there are different groups of invertebrates: invertebrates with segmented bodies, jointed legs, and hard outer coverings (arthropods); invertebrates with soft bodies (mollusks); invertebrates with spiny skin (echinoderms); worms (platyhelminthes, nematodes, annelids); invertebrates with stinging cells (cnidarians); and sponges (porifera). Let each student choose an invertebrate to research. Then have students complete *Invertebrate Investigation* (page 21) and share their findings with the class. This may work better as a homework assignment if encyclopedias and research materials are not readily available in your classroom.

Amazing Animals

Animals with backbones are called vertebrates. There are five main kinds of vertebrates.

Read the descriptions below. Then label each picture with the type of vertebrate.

Fish live in water and most are covered with scales. They breathe through gills and have fins that help them swim. Fish are cold-blooded, and the young hatch from eggs.

Amphibians usually live part of their life in water and part on land. Even if they spend most of their adult life on land, they often live near water. Amphibians do not have scales. They are cold-blooded, and most lay eggs in water.

Reptiles have dry scales or plates, and they spend all or much of their life on land. Reptiles are cold-blooded, and they lay eggs with leathery shells.

Birds are warm-blooded animals with feathers and wings. Birds lay hard-shelled eggs, and many build nests to protect their eggs.

Mammals are warm-blooded animals with hair. Almost all bear their young live, and the young drink mother's milk.

FS-23213 Science Made Simple ▪ © Frank Schaffer Publications, Inc.

Name _____

Invertebrate Investigation

Animals without backbones are called invertebrates (in-VER-teh-brates). Choose an invertebrate to investigate. Look in encyclopedias and books to find out information. Answer the questions below. Then draw a picture of your invertebrate.

1. What is the name of the invertebrate? _____

2. What does it look like? _____

   _____

3. Where does it live? _____

   _____

4. How does it move? _____

   _____

5. What does it eat? _____

6. Find out what classification group your invertebrate belongs to. Circle the group below.

   Arthropods   Mollusks

   Echinoderms   Platyhelminthes, Nematodes, Annelids

   Cnidarians   Porifera

7. Draw a picture of your invertebrate.

SCIENCE FAIR FUN

Class Activity

People often mix up certain animals. For example, some people think that spiders are a type of insect. Comparing the difference between insects and spiders can be an interesting science fair project. The presentation might include a display with drawings or photographs labeled to show differences such as main body parts and number of legs. In addition, students may include items easily collected for display, such as egg sacs, a spider web, and insect pupae.

To collect a spider web you will need aerosol paint (white is best); a sheet of stiff, black matte or construction paper; and brush-on paper glue. Once you have found a web that you want to save, check to be sure the web's owner is not close by, then spray the web lightly with paint. When the web is dry, spread a thin layer of glue on the black paper and press it carefully against the web. With your finger, clear away any supporting strands.

FASCINATING FACTS

Class Activity

Tell your students these fascinating facts about insects:

Insects are the only invertebrates that can fly.

The heaviest insect is the Goliath beetle of Africa. It can weigh almost a quarter of a pound.

The longest insect is the giant walkingstick of Indonesia. Some have been measured at a little more than a foot long.

Challenge your students to look in the encyclopedia to find other fascinating facts about insects.

LANGUAGE LINK

Class Activity

As a homework assignment, ask students to find at least three descriptive phrases that compare human behavior to animal behavior, such as *busy as a bee*, *quiet as a mouse*, and *clever as a fox*. Write all of the phrases on the board. Then lead the class in a discussion about how the animal's behavior led to the use of the phrase.

SPOTLIGHT ON SCIENTISTS

Class Activity

Give students copies of page 23 and ask them to read the story about Jane Goodall and answer the questions. Explain that animals behave differently in captivity than they do in the wild, and it is important that dedicated scientists observe creatures in their natural habitats. Then ask your students to choose an animal to study in their own community and write a brief report about it.

FS-23213 Science Made Simple ▪ © Frank Schaffer Publications, Inc.

Spotlight on Scientists

Jane Goodall was born in London, England, but her laboratory is the dense forest of Africa. Animals in zoos and parks do not act the same as they do in nature, so Jane Goodall spent many years watching chimpanzees in the wild. She began her work in 1960 at Gombe National Park in Tanzania. At first, the animals didn't trust her and stayed far away. After about a year, they became used to seeing her trailing after them with her notebook. Now, because of her bravery and hard work, we know that chimpanzees are very smart and that they can make and use simple tools. Sometimes they share food, and they even work together when they are hunting. Jane Goodall has given us a much clearer picture of how chimpanzees live.

Choose an animal you want to learn more about. Begin by answering these questions:

1. What animal would you like to learn about? _____

2. Where does that animal live? _____

3. What are some of the tools you will need for your study? _____

_____

4. What are some of the things you want to learn about your animal? _____

_____

5. What are some problems you might run into in your study?

_____

_____

Physical Science

The universe is made up of two things—matter and energy. Energy is the ability to do work, or more simply, energy is what makes things happen. Matter is anything that takes up space and has mass. Physical science introduces your students to some of the mysteries of science.

PHYSICAL SCIENCE RESOURCES

Books for Students

The Science Book of Magnets by Neil Ardley (Harcourt Brace Jovanovich, 1991). This book has plenty of photographs along with experiments and activities about magnetism.

The World of the Atom by Neil Ardley (Gloucester Press, 1989). This is an easy-to-understand book that covers everything from electrons to elements.

Experiments With Magnets by Helen Challand (Regensteiner Publishing Enterprises, 1986). Photographs guide the way for the simple experiments in this book.

The Usborne Science Encyclopedia by Annabel Craig and Cliff Rosney (Usborne Publishing, 1988). This is an encyclopedia of physical sciences made very appealing with colorful illustrations and plenty of interesting sidebars. The book includes a list of scientists and inventors, charts, tables, and a glossary.

Batteries, Bulbs, and Wires by David Glover (Kingfisher Books, 1993). Ideas for science fair projects and experiments on magnets and electricity can be found in this nicely illustrated book.

Electricity by Pam Robson (Aladdin Books, 1992). This book provides plenty of projects for students from electromagnets to circuits.

Web Sites

Discover Magazine (http://www.enews.com/magazines/discover)

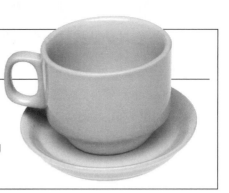

Matter

Matter is anything that takes up space and has mass. The three forms of matter are solid, liquid, and gas. Solids have a definite shape. Liquids and gases do not have a definite shape but do take up space. Use the following activities to give students a chance to learn about the states of matter.

DESCRIBING MATTER

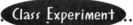
Class Experiment

Matter can be described in two ways. One is by its physical properties. Those are the things we can see and feel, such as the size, weight, shape, and smell of something. The other way is by chemical properties, or the way a substance reacts. This demonstration will illustrate the difference between the two.

Materials: a sheet of standard typing paper; a match; a fireproof container (such as a large ash tray); scissors; a bottle of water

What to Do: Begin by having students describe the piece of paper. Then ask a volunteer to cut the paper in half and then cut or tear one half into even smaller pieces. Show the pieces to the class and ask, *Although they are smaller than the original, would you still call the material paper? Do the pieces still feel and smell like the original? What is the physical property that was changed?* (size)

Now take the other half of the paper and carefully burn it in the ash tray. Keep a bottle of water close at hand in case of an emergency. When the paper has completely burned, ask students to look at the substance. Ask, *Is it still paper, or has it been changed to something else?* (ash) *How does it feel, sound, and smell now?* Explain that what took place when you burned the paper was a chemical reaction. One of the chemical properties of most paper is that it will burn.

INVISIBLE INK

Class Activity

Heat can bring about a chemical reaction in lemon juice that causes it to change color—a change that can also result in some fun.

Materials: a lemon cut in half; a small cup; a toothpick (or cotton swab); a lit candle; thin white paper

What to Do: Squeeze the juice from the lemon into the cup. Dip the toothpick or cotton swab into the juice and use it to write a message or draw a picture on the paper. Allow the juice to dry completely. Then hold the paper over the candle, being very careful not to get too close. The invisible message will soon become readable as the lemon juice turns a brown color.

LET'S EXPERIMENT: HEAVY AIR

Everything made of matter has mass. Mass is simply a measure of how much matter is present in an object. One way to measure the mass of something on Earth is to weigh it. To help students understand this, write on the board *Matter takes up space and has weight*. If you can, provide a scale and allow students to weigh various items and answer the questions *Does the object take up space? Does the object have weight?* Mention that even the air around us is made up of matter. Show that air takes up space by blowing up a balloon. Ask students if the balloon is bigger now than before it was inflated. Ask what is inside the balloon. When they answer air, explain that you used air from your lungs to inflate the balloon and that air is taking up space. This experiment will help to show that air has weight.

Materials: copies of pages 27–28 for each student or group; two large balloons; three 12-inch pieces of string; a plastic ruler; a sharp pin

What to Do: Tie one piece of string in the center of the ruler, using the six-inch mark as a guide. Tie the other end of the string to something, such as a light fixture, that will allow the ruler to hang horizontally. Blow up the two balloons to exactly the same size and tie a knot in each. Then tie a string to each. Hang one balloon from each end of the ruler, adjusting the strings to make the ruler level and the balloons completely balanced. This may take a little time to get just right. Finally, burst one balloon with the pin.

Results: When the two air-filled balloons are at each end of the ruler, it is balanced. When you burst one balloon, the air escapes and the weight of the air in the undamaged balloon pulls down on that side of the ruler. (Please note that technically this experiment shows that air compressed by the balloon has greater weight than an equal volume of air at standard atmospheric pressure, but for this grade level, you may simply say that it shows that air has weight.)

INVISIBLE FORCE

Here's another way to demonstrate the weight of air.

Materials: a full sheet of newspaper; a ruler; a large table or flat surface with an edge

What to Do: Spread the newspaper open so that one edge of the paper runs along the edge of the surface. Smooth it down so it is very flat. Slip the ruler under the newspaper so that about three inches of the ruler is sticking out over the edge. Ask a student to flip the paper up by slapping down hard on the ruler. Have another student try it, but this time by pressing very slowly on the ruler.

Results: The first student will find the task very difficult because air pressure is pushing down on the large sheet of paper, resisting the rapid movement. The slower-moving student allows air to get under the paper, equalizing the pressure. The paper moves easily.

Let's Experiment: Heavy Air

Problem:

Is air made up of matter?

What Do I Know?

Air takes up space.

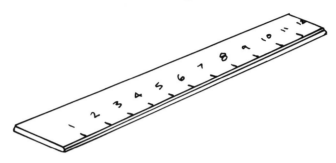

Question:

Does air have weight?

Materials:

two large balloons
a plastic ruler
three 12-inch pieces of string
a pin

Predict:

If two air-filled balloons are tied at each end of a ruler, the ruler is balanced. What do you think will happen if you burst one of the balloons? Write your prediction on your record sheet.

What to Do:

1. Tie one piece of string in the center of the ruler at the six-inch mark.

2. Tie the other end of the string so that the ruler will hang freely.

3. Blow up the two balloons to exactly the same size and knot them. Then tie a string to each.

4. Tie the loose end of each string to the ruler, one at the one-inch mark and one at the eleven-inch mark.

5. Adjust the strings until the ruler is perfectly balanced.

6. Use the pin to burst one balloon.

Collecting and Analyzing Information:

On your record sheet, write down what you observed.

Conclusion:

Do my results help to show that air has weight? How? Write your answers on your record sheet.

Let's Experiment: Heavy Air

Problem:
Is air made up of matter?

What Do I Know?
Air takes up space.

Question:
Does air have weight?

Predict:
What do you think will happen if you burst one of the balloons?

_____

_____

Collecting and Analyzing Information:
What happened when you burst one balloon?

_____

_____

Draw a picture showing what the ruler and balloons looked like after one of the balloons was popped.

```



```

Conclusion:
Does my experiment help to show that air has weight? How?

_____

_____

SOLIDS, LIQUIDS, AND GASES

Class Experiment

Matter can exist in three states: solid, liquid, and gas. Here is a way to demonstrate the difference.

Materials: a rock; a glass of water; a balloon; a small bowl

What to Do: On the board write:

A solid has a definite shape.
A liquid takes the shape of the container it is in.
A gas spreads out to take the shape of the container it is in.

Explain to your students that matter is made up of tiny building blocks called atoms. Sometimes the atoms join together in groups called molecules. There are many millions of molecules in a single drop of water. If the atoms in a substance are packed very tightly together, they make up a solid.

Show your students the rock. First, place it in the bowl. Then move it to the table. Ask, *Does the rock change its shape at any time?* Pour some water from the glass into the bowl. Ask, *Does the water change its shape?* Blow air (gas) into the balloon. Ask, *Does the air spread out to fill the container? What would happen if you tried to put the rock or the water in the balloon?* (The rock would not change shape. The water would take the shape of the balloon.)

MOLECULES ON THE MOVE

Class Activity

Put a few drops of red food coloring in a glass of water. As the color begins to disperse, explain to your students that the molecules in liquids are always moving so that eventually the molecules in the food coloring spread throughout the water. Time how long it takes for the water to turn red. Explain that molecules in gases move even faster than those in liquids. Standing in the front of the class, spray a small amount of floral room deodorizer into the air. Ask students to raise their hands as soon as they smell it. Time how long it takes before the students in the back row detect the scent.

LET'S EXPERIMENT: WATER IN THE AIR

Group Experiment

Water is an unusual substance because it exists on this planet in three states (solid, liquid, and gas). Your students can easily see water in its liquid and solid states. This experiment will show that there is water vapor in the air. A vapor is a gas given off by a liquid or a solid.

Materials: copies of pages 30–31 for each student or group; a large glass jar with a lid; enough ice cubes to fill the jar; a towel

What to Do: Students will fill the jar nearly to the top with ice and put the lid tightly on the jar. Then have the students dry the jar and place it in a warm spot, but not in direct sunlight, and wait for 15 minutes.

Results: Droplets of water will form on the outside of the jar. When warm, moist air touches something cold, the water vapor in the air collects into drops of liquid water, or condenses. Explain that dew is formed by the same process on grass and on other surfaces as the air near the ground cools at night.

Let's Experiment: Water in the Air

Problem:
Does water exist in three states of matter?

What Do I Know?
Water exists as a liquid and a solid (ice).

Question:
Does water exist as a gas?

Materials:
one large glass jar with a lid
ice
a dry towel

Predict:
Gases can be changed into liquids by cooling them. What do you think will happen if you cool the air around a jar of ice? Write your prediction on your record sheet.

What to Do:
1. Fill the jar nearly to the top with ice.

2. Put the lid on the jar.

3. Using the towel, dry the outside of the jar.

4. Place the jar in a warm spot but not in direct sunlight.

Collecting and Analyzing Information:
Check the jar after 15 minutes, then after 30 minutes. On your record sheet, write down what you observed.

Conclusion:
Do my results help to show that water exists as a gas? How? Write your answers on your record sheet.

FS-23213 Science Made Simple • © Frank Schaffer Publications, Inc

Let's Experiment: Water in the Air

Problem:
Does water exist in three states of matter?

What Do I Know?
Water exists as a liquid and a solid (ice).

Question:
Does water exist as a gas?

Predict:
What do you think will happen if you cool the air around a jar of ice?

_____

_____

Collecting and Analyzing Information:

First check: Time _____ What I saw _____

_____

Second check: Time _____ What I saw _____

_____

Why was it important that the outside of the jar be completely dry before the experiment?

_____

_____

Conclusion:
Do my results help to show that water exists as a gas? How?

_____

_____

_____

JUST FOR FUN

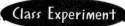
Class Experiment

The state of water can be changed by heating and cooling. An interesting way to demonstrate how is to do it in a closed system.

Materials: two glasses of the same size; duct or masking tape; water; ice; a small bowl; a sunny window

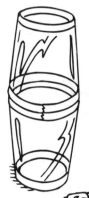

What to Do: Place a tablespoon of water in glass #1. Turn glass #2 over and place it on top so the glasses are rim to rim. Tape around the outside of the rims so that water vapor cannot escape. Place the glasses in a sunny window. Check them every so often. Once the water has evaporated, remove the glasses from the window. Don't remove the tape. Place the bottom of glass #1 in an ice-filled bowl.

Results: In the first stage of the experiment, the water will evaporate. In the second stage, it will condense.

Something More: This is the principle behind a terrarium. If possible, bring in a small terrarium for display. Students can even make their own from large plastic soda bottles, soil, and small plants.

BULLETIN BOARD IDEA

Class Activity

Make three labels, *Solid*, *Liquid*, and *Gas*, to go at the top of a bulletin board. Collect a variety of pictures from magazines that show substances in different states. Solids and liquids will be the easiest to find. For gases, you may have to be creative. They can be represented by balloons, neon signs, and pictures that show the results of air movement. Hold up each picture and ask students to identify the category it belongs in. Then let the students put the pictures where they belong on the bulletin board.

LANGUAGE LINK

Class Activity

Ask students to discover ways we use the states of matter in our language to express ideas. For example, what does it mean to *blow off steam* or *to be cold as ice* or *solid as a rock*? Have students find other examples.

ANOTHER CHANGE

Group Activity

Matter usually expands when it is warmed and contracts when it is cooled. This is because as something gets hotter, the atoms and molecules that it consists of start moving faster and bump into each other, causing them to spread out and take up more space. When the substance is cooled, the atoms and molecules slow down and can stay closer together. The physical exercise described below can help students remember this concept. You'll need room for your students to move around so, if possible, do it outside.

Divide the class into groups of about 10 students each. Tell them that they are atoms in a cold solid. Have them stand as close to each other as possible, and each turn very slowly around. Now tell them you're adding heat and have them move faster and faster. The group will then have to spread out or expand.

EXPANDING AIR

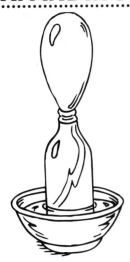

This demonstration will show that air expands when heated.

Materials: a plastic soda bottle; a balloon; a bowl; ice water; hot water

What to Do: Chill the soda bottle by filling it with very cold water. Pour the water out and slip the opening of the balloon over the open top. Stand the bottle up in a bowl of hot water.

Results: As the air in the bottle warms, it will expand, and the balloon will fill up.

Something More: Ask students what they think would happen if they put an inflated balloon in a freezer.

CONTRACTION

This experiment helps to show that air contracts when chilled.

Materials: a plastic soda bottle with a screw-on cap; a plastic bag; a rolling pin; ice; warm water

What to Do: Fill the bottle with warm water, cap it tightly, and let it set for a few minutes. Put 10 or 12 pieces of ice in the plastic bag and use the rolling pin to crush them small enough to fit into the bottle. When the ice is ready, quickly uncap the bottle, pour out the water, and shake in the ice. Cap the bottle tightly once again and wait.

Results: As the air inside the bottle cools, it contracts and takes up less space. The amount of time will vary, but eventually the pressure of the warmer air outside of the bottle will cause the bottle to crumple.

LET'S EXPERIMENT: AN EXCEPTION TO THE RULE

Unlike other substances, water expands when it freezes into ice. Unless you have access to a freezer, students will need to do this experiment at home.

Materials: copies of pages 34–35 for each student or group; a coffee can with a lid; a bottle cap; three pencils; two heavy-duty rubber bands; tape; water; a helper

What to Do: Fill the coffee can to the brim with cold water and cover it. Put the can on top of two pencils and tape them solidly to the bottom of the can. Put the bottle cap in the center of the lid and lay the third pencil on the cap. Use tape or rubber bands to hold the three pencils together at the point ends and again at the eraser ends. The top pencil should not be able to move. Place the can in the freezer overnight.

Results: The water will expand when it freezes and the pencil on the top of the can will break.

Let's Experiment: An Exception to the Rule

Problem:
What happens when water freezes?

What Do I Know?
Things contract when they freeze.

Question:
Does water contract when it freezes?

Materials:
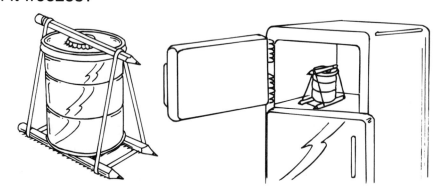
one coffee can with a lid
a bottle cap
three pencils
two heavy rubber bands
tape

Predict:
Most things contract, or get smaller, when they freeze. Does liquid water follow the same rules when it becomes ice? Write your prediction on your record sheet.

What to Do:
1. Fill the coffee can to the top with water and put the lid on it.

2. Tape two pencils securely to the bottom of the can.

3. Put the bottle cap in the center of the lid and place the third pencil on top of it.

4. Have your helper help you to use tape or rubber bands to hold the three pencils together as shown. Be sure the top pencil can't move.

5. Put the can in the freezer overnight.

Collecting and Analyzing Information:
Check the can in the morning. On your record sheet, write down what you observed.

Conclusion:
Do my results help to show that water expands or contracts when it freezes? How? Write your answers on your record sheet.

FS-23213 Science Made Simple ▪ © Frank Schaffer Publications, Inc.

Let's Experiment: An Exception to the Rule

Problem:

What happens when water freezes?

What Do I Know?

Things contract when they freeze.

Question:

Does water contract when it freezes?

Predict:

Does liquid water contract (get smaller) when it becomes ice?

_____

_____

Collecting and Analyzing Information:

Time _____ What I saw _____

_____

_____

Conclusion:

Does water expand or contract when it freezes? How do you know?

_____

_____

_____

_____

Think About It:

Fill a glass with water and several ice cubes. Will the glass overflow when the ice melts?

_____

Magnets

Children are naturally curious about the amazing power of magnets. Use the following activities to give your students an opportunity to discover such things as why magnets attract only objects made of iron and steel or why magnets are stronger at their poles than between their poles.

DISCOVERY: MAGNETIC ATTRACTION

Group Activity

Introduce your students to magnetism with this discovery activity.

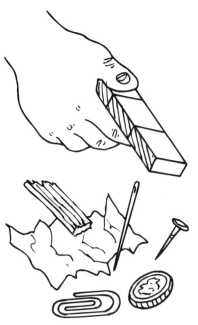

Materials: a copy of page 37 for each student; four of each of these items: bar magnets; pieces of aluminum foil; pennies; steel nails; pencils; paper clips; sewing needles; thin pieces of wood; pieces of paper; nickels; small mirrors

What to Do: Divide the class into four groups and let each group conduct its own discovery. Have students predict which items will be attracted to the magnets and which will not. Have them write their predictions on the activity sheet. Have students take turns passing the magnets over the items to test their guesses. Then have them separate the items into two groups—*magnetic* and *not magnetic*—and complete the activity sheet.

Results: The objects that contain iron or steel will attract a magnet.

Something More: Have the students try the same thing while holding wood, paper, or glass between a magnet and an object.

DISCOVERY: FIELD OF FORCE

Class Activity

Allow your students to discover the magnetic field around a magnet with this activity.

Materials: a copy of page 38 for each student; iron filings or bits cut from a steel scouring pad (no soap); a bar magnet; a horseshoe magnet; a sheet of thin cardboard

What to Do: Explain to your students that there is an area around a magnet called the magnetic field. Although it is invisible to the eye, there is a way for your students to see it for themselves. Place the bar magnet on a flat surface. Sprinkle iron filings on the cardboard and hold it just above the magnet, without actually touching it. Let your students predict what they think will happen and record their predictions on their activity sheets. Then tap the cardboard lightly until you see a pattern in the filings. These lines are the lines of magnetic force that surround the magnet. Repeat the process using the horseshoe magnet. Have the students describe what happened on their activity sheets. If you want, you can preserve the pattern by spraying it with a spray-on adhesive.

Discovery: Magnetic Attraction

A magnet is an object that attracts certain materials, such as iron or steel. People have known about magnets for more than 2,000 years. The first magnets were natural rocks, called lodestones, found near a Greek town named Magnesia.

Your teacher has given you some objects to test. Which of them do you think will be attracted to the magnet? Write your prediction below.

My Prediction:

These are the objects that will be attracted to the magnet.

_____

_____

_____

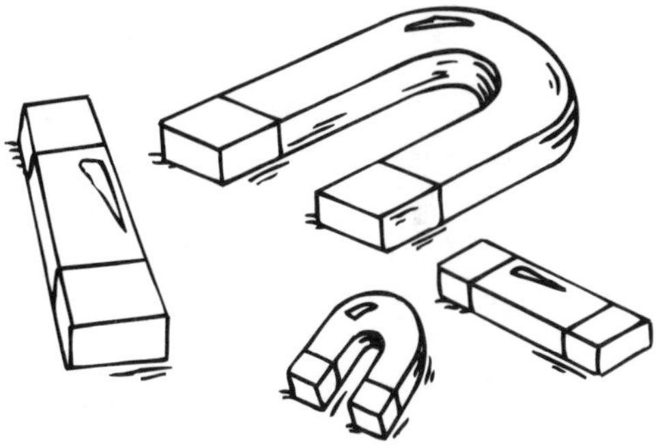

Now test each object.

Results:

These are the objects that were attracted to the magnet.

_____

_____

_____

_____

How are the objects that were attracted to the magnet alike?_____

_____

Think of a way to test what might happen if you try to block the magnetic

effect. Write your idea, and then try it._____

_____

_____

Discovery: Field of Force

There is an area around every magnet called the magnetic field. It is invisible to the eye, but here is a way you can see it for yourself.

Materials:
iron filings
a bar magnet
a sheet of thin cardboard

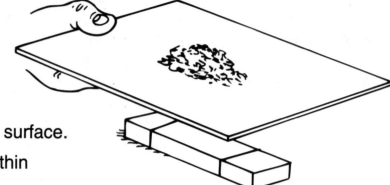

What to Do:
1. Place the bar magnet on a flat surface.

2. Sprinkle the iron filings on the thin cardboard.

3. Hold the cardboard just above the magnet, but don't touch it.

4. Tap the cardboard lightly.

Describe what happened.

_____

_____

_____

_____

_____

_____

_____

_____

_____

Draw a picture to show what happened.

FS-23213 Science Made Simple ▪ © Frank Schaffer Publications, Inc.

DISCOVERY: MAGNETIC FORCE

Let your students discover the behavior of magnetic poles with this activity.

Explain that the magnetic force of a magnet is strongest at the ends, called poles, and every magnet has a north and a south pole. Poles that are alike push each other away and unlike poles attract each other. Let students touch two magnets together, like poles first and then unlike poles, to discover what happens.

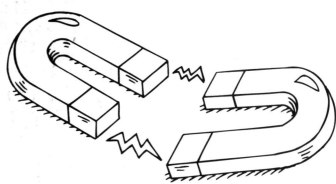

HOW MAGNETS FORM

This demonstration gives insight into how natural magnets form.

Materials: two dozen wooden matches; an iron nail; a paper clip

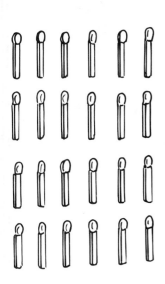

What to Do: Explain that a nonmagnetic iron is made up of tiny units each with its own north and south poles and that you are using matches to represent those units. The head of the match is the north pole, and the other end is the south pole. Drop the matches in a jumble on a table and let students see how the match heads face all different directions. Explain that if something (such as the effect of Earth's magnetism) causes the matches to line up, (turn the match heads to all face one direction) the iron becomes magnetized. Have a student volunteer try to attract the paper clip with the nail. Now rub the nail in one direction on the bar magnet about 30 times. Have the student try again.

Results: The first time, the nail will not attract the paper clip. By rubbing the nail across the magnet, you are aligning the molecules in the nail, and it will act temporarily as a magnet.

Something More: Let students try to magnetize the nail by rubbing in both directions. Let them discover what happens.

MAKING A COMPASS

This activity lets students make their own compasses.

Materials: copies of page 40 for each student or group; a thin slice of cork (one-half inch); a steel sewing needle; a bar magnet; dish soap; a clean, plastic margarine container

What to Do: Have students rub the needle across the bar magnet at least 30 times in one direction. Fill the container with water and place a drop of dish soap in the center. Float the cork slice on the dish soap. Then place the needle in the center of the cork (tape it if necessary). Spin it gently. When it stops, it will point north. Have students record on the activity sheet why they think compasses are useful.

Making a Compass

Planet Earth is something like a giant magnet. It has a magnetic field around it and a north and a south pole. About 5,000 years ago, a Chinese emperor named Huang-ti discovered that a magnetized bit of metal that was free to move would point north. Although he didn't understand what magnetism was, he had developed the first compass. You can make your own compass, too.

Materials:

a thin slice of cork
a steel sewing needle
a bar magnet
dish soap
a clean, plastic margarine container

What to Do:

1. Rub the sewing needle across the bar magnet at least 30 times in one direction.

2. Fill the margarine container with water.

3. Place a drop of dish soap in the center of the water.

4. Float the cork on the dish soap.

5. Place the needle on the cork.

6. Spin the cork very gently. When it stops spinning, it will point north.

   In what ways do you think compasses are useful?

   _____

   _____

   _____

   _____

   _____

FS-23213 Science Made Simple ▪ © Frank Schaffer Publications, Inc.

Art Link—On Stage

Art Project

Here's a fun thing to do with magnets. Have students make their own puppets.

Materials: a shoebox; thin cardboard; scissors; crayons; tape; paper clips; two bar magnets

What to Do: To make the stage, cut out one long side of the shoebox. Turn the box bottom-side up and make a one-inch cut into each corner of the side you cut out. Push the box lid into the slits and tape it in place. Decorate your stage.

Draw and cut out two puppets of any sort about one-inch high from the cardboard. Leave a tab on the bottom. Fold the tab under so that each puppet will stand up. Slip a paper clip onto the tab. Set your puppets on the stage. Slip your hand under the shoe box and use the bar magnets to move the puppets around.

THE MYSTERIOUS MAGNET

Class Activity

This demonstration will fascinate students because it looks almost like a magic trick.

Materials: a drinking glass; a long bar magnet; thread; a paper clip; tape

What to Do: Set the glass on a table and place the bar magnet across the top of it so that at least an inch extends over the edge of the glass. Tie about 10 inches of thread to the paper clip. Touch the free end of the paper clip lightly to the magnet so that it hangs from it. Very gently, pull down on the thread until the paper clip is still attracted, but there is space between it and the magnet. It may take a few tries to get it just right. Tape the end of the thread to the table. The clip will appear to defy gravity. (You might want to practice before doing the demonstration in front of the class.) Have students try slipping materials in between the magnet and the paper clip to see if they can interfere with the attraction.

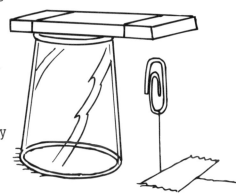

MAGNETIC MUSCLE

Class Experiment

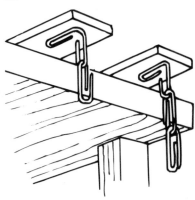

Some magnets have a stronger magnetic field than others. To demonstrate this, you will need three bar magnets of the same size and a handful of paper clips. Tape each magnet down flat on a table so they extend over the edge at least an inch. Be sure the magnets are far enough apart that they don't interfere with each other. Unbend one wire of one paper clip to form a sort of hook that will hold other paper clips. Lightly touch the "holder" paper clip to the underneath of the magnet, then start slipping on more clips to add weight. See how many each magnet can hold until it gives way.

Electricity

Electricity is a form of energy that we depend on in our daily lives. Use the following activities to give your students opportunities to learn about the mystery of electricity and the importance of it.

LET'S EXPERIMENT: WHAT IS STATIC ELECTRICITY?

Group Experiment

This experiment will let students discover one type of electricity—static electricity.

Materials: copies of pages 43–44 for each student or group; two balloons; a wool scarf or sweater; string

What To Do: Ask students if they have ever walked across a carpet and then gotten a shock when they touched a doorknob. Explain that what happened is static electricity. It is created when some kinds of objects are rubbed together and electric charges move from one object to another. Tell your students that you will be demonstrating the concept of static electricity.

First blow up and knot both balloons. Attach about 18 inches of string to each balloon. Holding the ends of the strings, touch the two balloons together. Now rub the balloons with the wool scarf. Touch the balloons together again.

Results: The first time you hang the balloons together, they are neutrally charged and will touch. By rubbing the balloons with the wool scarf, you are "knocking" electrons from the scarf, which pile up in the balloons, making them negatively charged. Because they are both negative, they will repel each other.

Something More: The balloons will attract things that are more positively charged than they are, such as a wall or the hair on a student's head. Try rubbing one balloon on a wall for one minute and the other for two minutes. Stick both to the wall. Then have the class keep track of which balloon drops first.

FUN WITH STATIC ELECTRICITY

Class Experiment

Here are some other fun things to do to show static electricity:

Dancing Butterflies: Cut out 10 small, simple paper butterflies. Rub a wool scarf across a hard plastic comb, then pass the comb over the butterflies without touching them. They will be attracted to the comb.

Shy Water: Rub a wool scarf across a plastic spoon, then hold the back of the spoon near a thin stream of water from a faucet.

An Impossible Task: Mix together a pinch of pepper and a pinch of salt on a piece of clean white paper. Tell your students you can separate some of the pepper from the salt without touching either substance. Rub a wool scarf across a hard plastic comb, then pass the comb over the salt and pepper. The pepper will be attracted to the comb, but the salt will not.

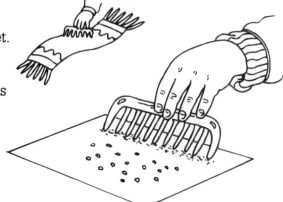

Let's Experiment: Static Electricity

Problem:
How does static electricity behave?

What Do I Know?
When electrons move from one thing to another, static charge can build up.

Question:
How do objects with like charges react to each other?

Materials:
two balloons
a wool scarf or sweater
string

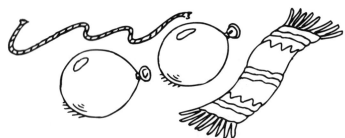

Predict:
By rubbing balloons with a wool scarf, you can "knock" electrons from the scarf. They will pile up in the balloons, making them negatively charged. How will two negatively charged balloons react to each other? Write your prediction on your record sheet.

What to Do:
1. Blow up and knot both balloons.
2. Attach 18 inches of string to each balloon.
3. Holding the ends of the two strings, touch the balloons.
4. Record what happens.
5. Rub both balloons with the wool scarf.
6. Repeat step #3.

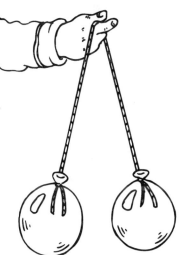

Collecting and Analyzing Information:
On your record sheet, write down what happens.

Conclusion:
Was my prediction correct? Write your answers on your record sheet.

Let's Experiment: Static Electricity

Problem:

How does static electricity behave?

What Do I Know?

When electrons move from one thing to another, static charge can build up.

Question:

How do objects with like charges react to each other?

Predict:

How will two negatively charged balloons react to each other?

_____

_____

Collecting and Analyzing Information:

First try to make the balloons touch. What happened?

_____

Next rub the balloons with a wool scarf. Try to make the balloons touch. What happened?

_____

Draw a picture to show what happened.

```



```

Conclusion:

Does my experiment show how two objects with like charges react to each other? Was my prediction correct?

_____

_____

Something More:

Try rubbing the balloons with different materials, like silk or cotton, to see what happens.

FS-23213 Science Made Simple ▪ © Frank Schaffer Publications, Inc.

ABOUT CURRENT ELECTRICITY

Class Activity

Explain to students that the electricity that provides light and runs machinery is called current electricity. Have students think of ways that they use electricity every day. Then have students study the cross section of a family home on page 46 and have them circle all of the ways that electricity is being used. When they are finished, conduct a tour of the classroom to find ways that electricity is being used there.

THE OLDEN DAYS

Class Activity

Ask for a volunteer to pretend to be someone visiting from 200 years in the past. Have the students try to describe to the visitor what electricity is.

Then have students write a short story about what their daily life would be like if there was no electricity. What would they have to do without? What would they use for light? What would they use for heat?

THE PATH OF ELECTRICITY

Class Activity

Explain to students that when electrons all flow in one direction, they form current electricity and the path they follow is called a circuit. If the path is continuous, the current will flow, but if the path is broken, the current stops. That's how a switch works. A piece of metal (usually copper) is in place when the switch is on. When the switch is off, the metal moves out of line and the circuit is broken.

Take apart an old flashlight with your class and examine the switch. Note where the flashlight comes in contact with the batteries and point out that a battery contains a store of chemical energy.

As a homework assignment, ask students to find out what a short circuit is.

SCIENCE FAIR FUN: BUILD A SWITCH

Class Experiment

This hands-on project can be an impressive entry in a science fair.

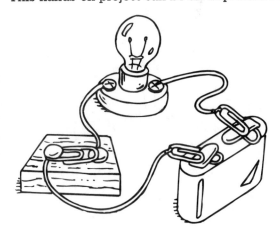

Materials: large dry cell battery; light bulb; socket; three 4-inch lengths of insulated copper wire; large paper clip; block of wood; two metal tacks; hammer

What to Do: Push one tack into one end of the block of wood and loop one end of the paper clip under it. Stop when about an eighth of an inch of the head still sticks up. About an inch away, push another tack into the wood in the same manner. The paper clip should be able to touch that tack, too, or be able to swing out of the way. That's the switch.

Strip about one-half inch of insulation from each end of the copper wires. Connect the end of one wire to the first tack and the other end to a battery terminal. Connect another wire from the other battery terminal to the socket. Connect the third wire from the socket to the second tack. Swing the paper clip so that it touches both tacks, and the bulb should light.

Electricity at Home

Electricity is a kind of energy. Many of the things you use every day need electricity to make them work. Look at the drawing of the home below. Circle all of the things you can find that use electricity.

FS-23213 Science Made Simple ▪ © Frank Schaffer Publications, Inc.

BULLETIN BOARD DISPLAY

Explain to students that electricity flows better though some materials (called conductors) than through others (called insulators). Divide the bulletin board into two halves. Label one side *Conductors* and the other side *Insulators*. Have students bring in pictures or samples of each to put on the board. Examples of conductors are gold, silver, copper, aluminum, and water. Examples of insulators are glass, rubber, cloth, wood, plastic, and air.

Conductors   Insulators

Art Project

*S*afety *W*ith *E*lectricity

Electrical energy can be dangerous and even deadly. Have students use page 48 to make their own Safety With Electricity posters. Encourage them to design their own symbols to illustrate the posters, such as cartoon lightning bugs. Before they begin, discuss safety and ask for ideas that you can write on the board. Below are some rules to mention if your students do not think of them on their own.

1. Never play with wall outlets or wall switches.

2. Never use the electricity from wall outlets to do experiments.

3. Do not touch a switch or an electric device when your hands are wet.

4. Stay away from power lines.

5. Do not use any electric devices in the bathtub, shower, or swimming pool.

6. Do not fly a kite or a model airplane near a power line.

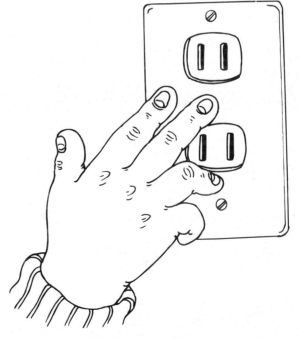

Something More: Put students in groups and have them act out the safety rules.

47

Name _____

 # $affety $With $Electricity

Electricity is an important part of everyday life, but it can be dangerous if it isn't handled safely. List 10 important safety rules to remember about electricity. Then draw a picture to illustrate one of the rules.

1. _____
2. _____
3. _____
4. _____
5. _____
6. _____
7. _____
8. _____
9. _____
10. _____

FS-23213 Science Made Simple • © Frank Schaffer Publications, Inc.

CONDUCTORS OR INSULATORS

Class Experiment ·······

Students can test for conductors or insulators by using the set up for the switch described on page 45. Leave the socket and battery hooked up, but remove the switch from the circuit so there are two bare wires. That is the test point. Try touching the bare wires to various materials to see if the circuit will be completed. For example, a penny will complete the circuit and the bulb will light. A glass marble will not complete the circuit.

MAKING AN ELECTROMAGNET

Class Activity ·······

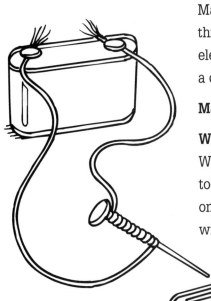

Magnetism and electricity are related. An electrical current traveling through a wire can create a magnetic field. A magnet that works by electricity is called an electromagnet. Here is how to build a classroom model.

Materials: dry cell battery; iron nail; three feet of thin speaker wire

What to Do: Scrape the insulation from about an inch of wire at each end. Wind the center of the wire around the nail, the more coils and the closer together they are the stronger the magnet. Attach one end of the wire to one battery terminal. Then attach the other to the other terminal. The nail will become a magnet. Try picking up paper clips. Detach one wire, and the magnetism stops. The electrical current traveling through the wire creates a magnetic field—a phenomenon known as electromagnetism.

THE BATTERY

Class Activity ·······

Explain to students that a battery is a store of chemical energy. In 1799, Alessandro Volta stacked small plates of silver and zinc alternately, with strips of blotting paper between them soaked in acid. Amazingly, an electric current flowed between the plates, and the first battery had been developed.

Make a classroom display of different types of batteries and the things that run on them.

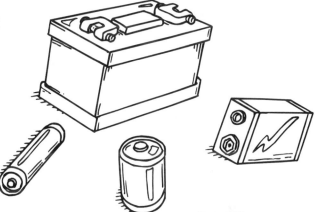

LANGUAGE LINK

Class Activity ·······

A unit of electrical force is called a volt and is named after Alessandro Volta. Ask students if they can find examples of other terms named after famous scientists. For example, electric current is measured in amperes (André Marie Ampère). Resistance is measured in units called ohms (Georg Simon Ohm).

Earth Science

Earth science includes the study of our home planet and our neighbors in the solar system. By introducing your students to Earth science, you will help them discover the universe around them.

CONCEPTS

In the following section, your students will discover:

- Earth's atmosphere is all around us even though you can't see it.

- Weather is the conditions occurring in the lower atmosphere at a given place.

- Climate is the average weather in an area over many years.

- The water cycle is one of the biggest recycling projects on Earth.

- The solar system is made up of the sun, the nine planets, and other satellites.

- The sun is a star and is the closest star to Earth.

- The moon appears to change over the course of a month.

EARTH SCIENCE RESOURCES

Books for Students

The Magic School Bus: Lost in the Solar System by Joanna Cole (Scholastic, 1990). This book lets your students accompany Miss Frizzle on an unexpected tour of the solar system.

Weather by Anita Ganeri (Franklin Watts, 1993). Information and activities on the atmosphere, wind patterns, precipitation, and weather forecasting can be found in this book.

Weather and Climate by Barbara Taylor (Kingfisher Books, 1993). This book provides experiments on weather patterns, violent weather, air pressure, and heat and cold along with clear illustrations.

Astronomy for Every Kid by Janice VanCleave (John Wiley & Sons, 1991). There are 101 simple experiments covering planets, the moon, the stars, and space travel in this fun book.

Night Sky by Carole Stott (Dorling Kindersley, 1993). Simple activities and a guide to observing stars and planets are found in this book.

Web Sites

National Hurricane Center (http://www.nhc.noaa.gov/)

National Climatic Data Center (http://www.ncdc.noaa.gov/ncdc.html)

The Earth's Atmosphere

Although you can't see it, smell it, or taste it, Earth's atmosphere is all around us. By introducing your students to the following activities, they'll discover the factors and conditions that affect our atmosphere.

WEATHER AND CLIMATE
Class Activity

Make two columns on the board. Label one *Weather* and the other *Climate*. Explain to students that weather is the variety of conditions occurring in the lower atmosphere (troposphere) at any given place. That's generally within seven miles of the surface of the planet. In the first column, write examples of weather, such as daily temperature, moisture in the air, and wind speed. Point out that weather can change in hours or stay the same for weeks.

In the second column, write examples of climate, such as annual rainfall, average summer temperature, and average humidity. Explain that climate is the average weather in an area over many years. Then give more examples of each and ask students to decide which ones describe weather and which ones describe climate. Some possibilities are a snowstorm; long, dry summers; partly cloudy; good growing season; foggy mornings in winter; light rain today; 22 inches of rain per year; and tornado warning.

THE FORECAST
Class Activity

If you can, bring a portable radio to school. Have the class listen to a weather report. Bring in an example of a weather map from a newspaper and review it together. Ask students to think of why it is important to know about the weather. Some reasons are so you can figure out what to wear and how to plan your day; so navigators on ships and planes can plan safe trips; so farmers know what and when to plant so people can be forewarned of storms and other dangers, such as possible flooding.

BULLETIN BOARD IDEA
Class Experiment

To track a month of local weather, pin a large calendar on the board or draw a calendar. As a homework assignment, have students listen to the weather report each night. Each day, record the previous day's weather conditions on the calendar. Ask students to notice any patterns that develop.

LANGUAGE LINK
Class Activity

There are many old sayings and poems about the weather that have become very colorful additions to our language. Give students several examples. Then ask them to find examples of their own. Try to find the scientific reasoning (if any) behind them.

Some examples are
- Red sky at night, sailor's delight. Red sky in the morning, sailor take warning.
- March comes in like a lion and goes out like a lamb.
- Ring around the moon, rain by noon.

THE WATER CYCLE

Explain to students that one of the biggest recycling projects on Earth is nature's own water cycle. Ask students to read about the water cycle and complete page 53.

Here is one way to make a classroom model of the water cycle.

Materials: metal pie plate; ice; water; tea kettle; hot plate; mitt

What to Do: Put ice in the pie plate. Put about two inches of water in the kettle and place it on the hot plate. Wearing a protective mitt, hold the pan about six inches above the kettle.

Results: The water boils, turning to steam and water vapor. Water vapor condenses on the bottom of the cold pie plate and forms drops that "rain" to the surface.

BULLETIN BOARD IDEA—CLOUDS

The best way to start a discussion of clouds is to go outside and observe them if possible. There are three main types, and scientists have described a number of combinations of these three. They are classified according to their height from the ground measured from the lowest point of the cloud.

Cirrus clouds are the highest. They look thin and wispy.

Cumulus clouds are light, fluffy-looking clouds.

Stratus cloud are low, often gray clouds that blanket the whole sky.

Create a bulletin board with pictures of all different kinds of clouds. In the center, pin a listing of the types of clouds so that students can determine which are pictured.

LET'S EXPERIMENT: FOG

Fog is simply a ground-hugging cloud. Have your students create their own fog in a bottle.

Materials: copies of pages 54–55 for each student or group; clear plastic soda bottle; a large ice cube; very warm water; plastic wrap

What to Do: First fill the bottle with very warm water to heat the air inside. Let it set for a moment, then pour out most of the water, leaving about an inch in the bottle. Place the ice cube over the opening of the bottle.

Results: The warm air in the bottle contains water vapor that cools on contact with ice. The water vapor condenses into tiny droplets that look much like fog.

Something More: Ask students to predict what would happen if they first wrapped the ice in plastic wrap.

Name _____

The Water Cycle

First read the story below. Then complete this picture of the water cycle by cutting out each label at the bottom of the page and gluing it in the proper place.

Earth is often called the water planet. There is water in the lakes, oceans, rivers, and ice caps. There is also water vapor in the air. None of Earth's water drifts off into space. In fact, the water that is falling as rain today has probably fallen billions of times before in part of a great cycle called the water cycle. First, the heat from the sun causes water to dry up (evaporate) and turn into water vapor. When water vapor rises, it cools in the atmosphere, forms drops, and falls again as rain.

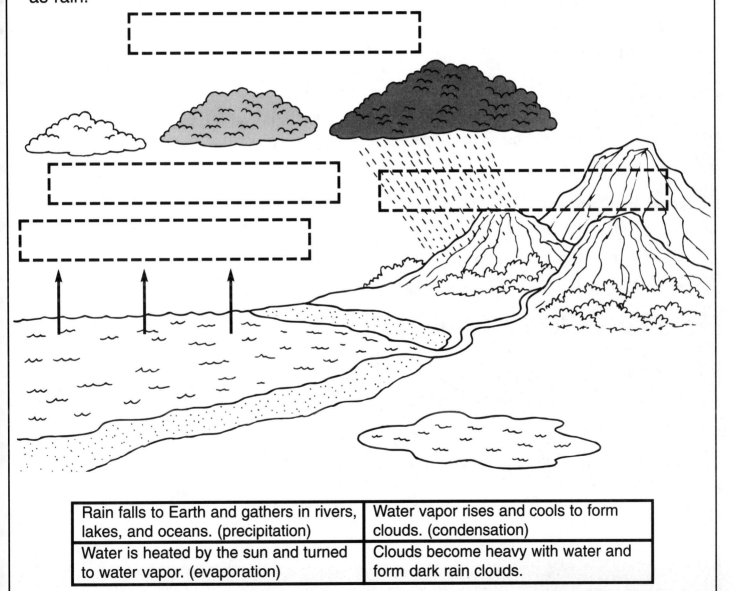

Rain falls to Earth and gathers in rivers, lakes, and oceans. (precipitation)	Water vapor rises and cools to form clouds. (condensation)
Water is heated by the sun and turned to water vapor. (evaporation)	Clouds become heavy with water and form dark rain clouds.

Let's Experiment: Fog

Problem:
What causes fog to form?

What Do I Know?
Water vapor condenses when the air cools.

Question:
Will fog form when warm and cold air meet?

Materials:
a clear one-liter soda bottle
warm water
a large ice cube

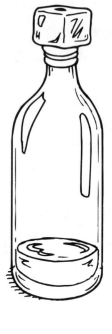

Predict:
Fog is a ground-hugging cloud. What do you think will happen if warm air in a bottle meets cool air at the top of the bottle? Write your prediction on your record sheet.

What to Do:
1. Fill the bottle with warm water to warm the air inside. Let it sit for a moment.

2. Pour out most of the water, leaving about an inch in the bottom.

3. Place the ice cube over the opening at the neck of the bottle.

Collecting and Analyzing Information:
Check the bottle every 5 minutes for 15 minutes. On your record sheet, write down what you see.

Conclusion:
Does my experiment help to show that fog can form when warm and cold air meet? How? Write your answers on your record sheet.

Let's Experiment: Fog

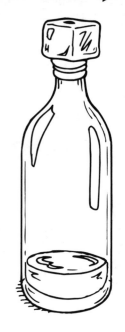

Problem:
What causes fog to form?

What Do I Know?
Water vapor condenses when the air cools.

Question:
Will fog form when warm and cold air meet?

Predict:
What do you think will happen if warm air in a bottle meets cool air at the top of the bottle?

_____

_____

Collecting and Analyzing Information:

First check: Time _____ What I saw_____

_____

Second check: Time _____ What I saw_____

_____

Third check: Time _____ What I saw_____

_____

Conclusion:
Does my experiment help to show that fog can form when warm and cold air meet? How?_____

_____

_____

Something More:
Do you think fog will still form if you cover the ice with plastic wrap?

_____

MATH LINK

The greatest rainfall in one year occurred in Cherrapunji, India, in 1861. The area received 1,042 inches of rain. Ask students to figure out the following: *How many feet of rain fell on Cherrapunji? If the rain fell evenly every day for the whole year, how much would have fallen each day? The usual annual rainfall in Cherrapunji was 425 inches. How much more did this town get than usual? Find out the average annual rainfall in your town.*

BAKED RAIN

Here is a way to measure the size of drops on a rainy day. Fill a shallow pan with about one-half inch of flour. Cover the pan with a plate. Run outside in the rain and uncover the pan for a couple of seconds until the drops form little balls of dough. Let the balls dry for a couple of hours. If possible, oven bake them at a low temperature until they harden. Sieve the hardened drops from the flour and measure them.

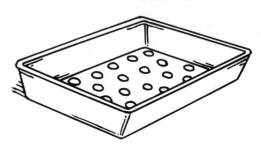

NATURE'S WAY

Tell your students that it isn't always easy to predict rain, but sometimes a pine cone can help. During warm, dry weather, a pine cone will open. It will usually close its scales snugly if rain is on the way. Have your students look for pine cones to use to predict if rain will be coming soon.

AFTER THE RAIN

Ask students if they have ever seen a rainbow. Explain that if you are standing with the sun behind you and there is moisture in the air, you could see a rainbow. Sunlight passes through millions of raindrops. The light is bent as it enters and leaves the drops. This causes white light to separate into its seven colors. Each color reaches your eye from a different angle and you see a rainbow.

Help students remember the colors of a rainbow in order with this name:

ROY G. BIV (top to bottom) red, orange, yellow, green, blue, indigo, violet.

To make a rainbow, fill a glass with water and place it on the window sill so sunlight passing through it will reach the floor. Place a large sheet of white paper on the floor. Move the glass around until the rainbow appears on the paper.

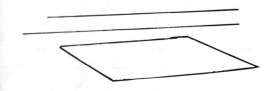

BULLETIN BOARD IDEA

Class Activity

Put together a display of many types of precipitation including magazine pictures of rain, dew, snow, frost, and hail. Ask students to add pictures or drawings to the board, as well as fun facts and records about each type of precipitation. For example, greatest snowfall, heaviest hailstone, and so forth.

A similar bulletin board can be prepared for types of storms, featuring tornadoes, hurricanes, and thunderstorms.

LANGUAGE LINK **Class Activity**

Many instruments used to measure the weather end in *meter* which is a Greek word that means "measure." Ask students if they can guess what each of the instruments listed below measures. To make it easier, put the choices on the board and have the class match each one to its instrument.

Thermometer—temperature
Barometer—air pressure
Anemometer—wind speed
Hygrometer—humidity or moisture in the air

Art Project

Art Smart—Storm Safety

Discuss safety measures that should be taken during severe storms. For example, don't stand under a tree during a storm, since lightning tends to strike tall objects. Or try not to use a telephone or electrical appliance during a thunderstorm. Have students draw pictures to demonstrate safety in severe weather.

MAKING A BAROMETER **Class Experiment**

Students can make a barometer to test the air pressure in their own neighborhoods.

Materials: a large glass jar; a balloon; a plastic straw; a plain white card; glue

What to Do: Cut a piece of material from the balloon. Stretch it over the top of the jar and secure it in place with the rubber band. Put a drop of glue in the center of the balloon material and attach the straw horizontally by one end. Keep the jar on a tabletop near a wall. Pin the white card next to the jar as shown. When the air pressure is high, it will push down on the balloon, causing the straw "indicator" to point to high.

DISCOVERY: SEEING SPARKS

Class Experiment

Have students use page 59 to create their own lightning.

Materials: a copy of page 59 for each student; a lightweight, tin baking tray; a large plastic bag; a handful of modeling clay; a small metal object such as a key; a wooden tabletop

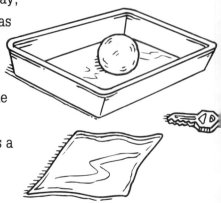

What to Do: In a darkened room, place the metal object on a wooden tabletop. Stick the modeling clay to the center of the tray and, touching the clay only, rub the bottom of the tray vigorously on the plastic bag for a moment or two. This will build up static electricity. Now, using the clay as a handle, pick up the tray and hold it near the metal object on the table.

Results: A small spark should jump from the tray to the metal object.

MATH LINK

Class Activity

We see a flash of lightning as soon as it happens because light travels so quickly. Sound travels much slower than light—about one mile in five seconds. Students can use this fact to figure out how far away lightning is. To do this, start counting seconds as soon as you see the flash. Count slowly (*one thousand one, one thousand two,* and so on). Stop when you hear thunder and divide the number you reached by five. That is how many miles away the lightning struck. For example, if you counted to five, the lightning was one mile away.

MOVING AIR

Class Experiment

Wind is the movement of air. The main cause of global air movement is the uneven heating of Earth's surface by the sun. To demonstrate this, shine a flashlight (the sun) on a globe or a soccer ball (the Earth). The area in the direct line of the beam gets the most light and warmth. As warm air rises, cooler air moves in to take its place. This demonstration will show that warm air rises.

Materials: white paper; a pencil; a candle; clay; scissors

What to Do: Cut the paper in a spiral as shown. Place a ball of clay at the edge of a table, and stick the eraser end of the pencil down into the clay so the pencil stands. Balance the spiral on the point of the pencil. Light the candle and hold it a couple of inches under the spiral.

Results: As the warmed air around the candle rises, it will cause the spiral to turn.

SPOTLIGHT ON SCIENTISTS

Class Activity

Give your students copies of page 60 and ask them to read the story about Joanne Simpson and answer the questions. Explain that at the time she first began her work, women did not have the same opportunities that they have today. Ask students to think of some of the jobs women do today that they were barred from in the past.

Discovery: **S**eeing **S**parks

Lightning is caused by the same sort of static electricity that makes your hair crackle when you comb it. Lightning strikes when there are unlike charges of electricity within a cloud, between a cloud and the ground, or between two clouds. Lightning is nature's way of making the charges equal.

Here is a way to make your own lightning.

Materials:

a lightweight, tin baking tray
a large plastic bag
modeling clay
a metal object (perhaps a key)
wooden tabletop

What to Do:

1. Place the metal object and the plastic bag on a wooden table.

2. Stick a large ball of clay into the center of the tray.

3. Holding the clay only, rub the tray quickly back and forth on the plastic bag for a moment or two.

4. Pick up the tray and hold it near the metal object.

Describe what happened.

_____

_____

_____

_____

Fun Fact:

At this very moment, there are thunderstorms raging in places all around the globe. There are about 6,000 flashes of lightning on Earth every second.

𝒮potlight on 𝒮cientists

Joanne Simpson was a student at the University of Chicago when the United States entered World War II in 1941. The armed forces desperately needed meteorologists (people who study the atmosphere and weather conditions) to help plan air travel during the war. Joanne Simpson helped to train military personnel, but when the war was over, she had a difficult time finding a position as a meteorologist. At that time women were not considered right for such a career. Finally, in 1960, Joanne Simpson was made a full professor of meteorology at the University of California at Los Angeles. One focus of her work was on cloud seeding. She also worked on the development of a method to help hurricanes to lose some of their force by using special flares.

What is something you would like to learn about the weather in your own community? Begin by answering these questions:

1. What weather condition do you want to learn about? _____

2. How often does this weather condition happen? _____

   _____

3. How does the weather condition affect you? _____

   _____

4. How does the weather condition affect your community? _____

   _____

5. What are some of the tools you will need for your study? _____

   _____

Something More: Rain won't form unless there are particles in the air for droplets to condense on. Cloud seeding is when artificial particles are sprayed into the clouds by airplanes. Seeding only works with clouds that might produce rain anyway.

FS-23213 Science Made Simple ▪ © Frank Schaffer Publications, Inc

WHICH WAY?

Class Activity

If you have a compass, it's easy to figure out which way the wind is blowing. But if you don't, just toss a little dust or grass in the air. The wind is described by the direction from which it blows. For example, a westerly wind blows from west to east.

TORNADO IN A BOTTLE

Class Experiment

For sheer power, tornadoes are the most destructive storms on Earth. Here is how to create a tornado in a bottle to demonstrate the funnel form of such storms.

Materials: two plastic one-liter soda bottles; water; food coloring or glitter; masking tape

What to Do: Fill one bottle about three-quarters full of water and pour in a few drops of food coloring or a teaspoon of glitter (or both). Tape the tops of the bottles together securely with masking tape. Turn the bottles so the empty one is on the bottom. With a good grip on the joined bottlenecks, swirl both bottles in a circular motion, then set on a flat surface.

Results: A funnel of water should form as the water from the full bottle drains into the empty one.

LET'S EXPERIMENT: COLD AIR

Group Experiment

Have students do this experiment to show that cool air sinks.

Materials: copies of pages 62–63 for each student or group; an oatmeal box; a thermometer; two pencils; salt; a plastic bag; ice

What to Do: Place the thermometer in the box and take a reading. Then leave it in the box. Fill the plastic bag with ice. Throw in a little salt because salt lowers the freezing point of water. Seal the bag. Place the pencils across the open top of the oatmeal box. Balance the ice-filled bag on the pencils. Check the temperature after 10 minutes and then again after 20 minutes.

Results: The air chilled by the ice will sink to the bottom of the oatmeal box and significantly lower the temperature.

MORE COLD AIR

Class Experiment

Here's another simple demonstration to show that cold air sinks. One day before the demonstration, make ice cubes with food coloring in them. With students, put an ice cube in a glass of room temperature water. As the ice melts, the cold, colored water sinks to the bottom to form a distinct layer.

Let's Experiment: Cold Air

Problem:
How does cold air behave?

What Do I Know?
Warm air rises.

Question:
Does cold air sink?

Materials:
one oatmeal box
a thermometer
two pencils
salt
a plastic bag
ice

Predict:
Warm air tends to expand and so becomes lighter. Cold air tends to contract. Does it become heavier? Write your prediction on your record sheet.

What to Do:
1. Place the thermometer in the oatmeal box and record the temperature. Leave it in the box.

2. Fill the plastic bag with ice, throw in a pinch of salt, and seal it.

3. Place the pencils across the opening of the oatmeal box.

4. Balance the ice-filled bag on the pencils.

Collecting and Analyzing Information:
Check the temperature after 10 minutes, then after 20 minutes. On your record sheet, write down what you see.

Conclusion:
Does my experiment help to show that cold air sinks? How? Write your answers on your record sheet.

FS-23213 Science Made Simple ▪ © Frank Schaffer Publications, Inc

Let's Experiment: Cold Air

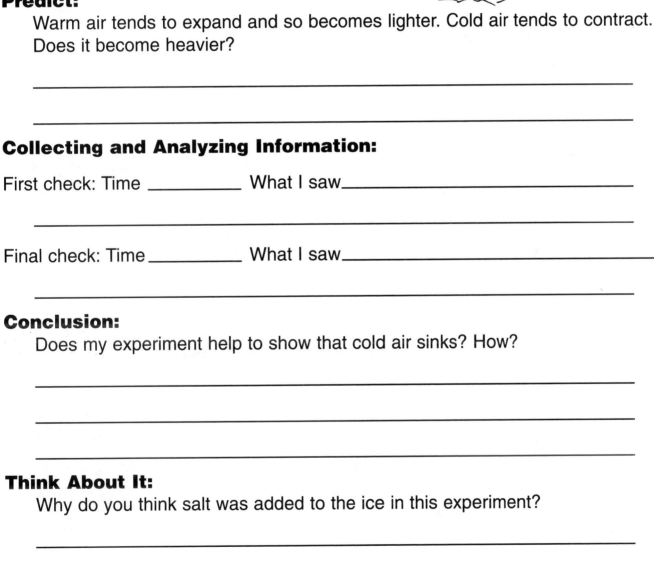

Problem:
How does cold air behave?

What Do I Know?
Warm air rises.

Question:
Does cold air sink?

Predict:
Warm air tends to expand and so becomes lighter. Cold air tends to contract. Does it become heavier?

_____

_____

Collecting and Analyzing Information:

First check: Time _____ What I saw_____

_____

Final check: Time _____ What I saw_____

_____

Conclusion:
Does my experiment help to show that cold air sinks? How?

_____

_____

Think About It:
Why do you think salt was added to the ice in this experiment?

_____

_____

LET'S EXPERIMENT: UNEVEN HEAT

Sand, soil, air, and water are all affected differently by the heat of the sun. This experiment will allow students to figure out which material absorbs heat more quickly and which holds it longer.

Materials: copies of pages 65–66 for each student or group; a bright light; two bowls or jars; two alcohol thermometers; a measuring cup; water; dry, dark soil

What to Do: Put one cup of soil in one bowl, and one cup of water in the other. Place a thermometer in each sample so the bulbs are just covered. Let the experiment stand in a shaded spot until both bowls are at room temperature. Place the bowls in direct sunlight or in the heat of a bright lamp for one hour. Record the temperature every 15 minutes.

Results: Soil should heat up faster than water. Have students test which loses heat faster.

THE COLOR FACTOR

This will demonstrate how color can affect heat absorption.

Materials: two coffee cans with lids; white paint; black paint; paint brushes; two alcohol thermometers; a sunny spot

What to Do: Have students paint the two coffee cans, one black and one white. Next, they fill the cans with water, place a thermometer in each, and set them in direct sunlight for one hour.

Results: The water in the black can will be hotter. Black absorbs sunlight while white reflects it. Ask students what color clothing would be the most comfortable on a hot day. Have students find out about cultures in hot climates. Have them determine what sort of clothes the people who live in these climates wear.

MATH LINK—NATURE'S WAY

If you don't have a thermometer, you can get help from a cricket to determine air temperature. Simply count the number of chirps the cricket makes in 15 seconds. Then add 37 to that number. You'll be fairly close.

Let's Experiment: Uneven Heat

Problem:

How does heat from the sun affect the ocean and the land?

What Do I Know?

Not all materials absorb heat the same.

Question:

Which absorbs heat from the sun faster, water or land?

Materials:

two glass bowls or jars
two thermometers
a measuring cup
dry, dark soil
water
a bright light or sunny spot

Predict:

Some substances absorb heat more quickly than others. Some release heat more quickly than others.
Will water or soil heat up faster? Write your prediction on your record sheet.

What to Do:

1. Put one cup of soil in one bowl and one cup of water in the other.

2. Place a thermometer in each sample so the bulbs are just covered.

3. Put the experiment in a shady spot until both samples are at room temperature.

4. Place both bowls in the sun (or under a lamp) for an hour.

Collecting and Analyzing Information:

Check the temperature every 15 minutes. On your record sheet, write down what you see.

Conclusion:

Which heats faster, soil or water? Was your prediction correct? Write your answers on your record sheet.

Let's Experiment: Uneven Heat

Problem:
How does heat from the sun affect the ocean and the land?

What Do I Know?
Not all materials absorb heat the same.

Question:
Which absorbs heat from the sun faster, water or land?

Predict:
Will water or soil heat up faster?

Collecting and Analyzing Information:

First check: Time _____ What I saw _____

_____

Second check: Time _____ What I saw _____

_____

Third check: Time _____ What I saw _____

_____

Final check: Time _____ What I saw _____

_____

Conclusion:
Which heats faster, soil or water? Was your prediction correct?

_____

_____

Something More:
Try this experiment using different materials, such as salt water and beach sand.

The Solar System

Children are naturally curious about the solar system. It is made up of the sun, the nine planets, and other satellites. Use the following activities to help your students discover the fascinating features of our solar system.

THE VIEW FROM EARTH

Class Activity .....

The movements of planet Earth make it appear that the sun and moon travel across the sky from east to west. Explain to your class that it is actually the Earth that is turning, or rotating, from west to east. Students can observe the apparent motion of the sun by going outside and noting the sun's position (without staring directly at it) and then going outside an hour later and noting its position again. The sun will be moving across the sky.

THE SEASONS

Class Activity .....

To show students why we have seasons, you'll need a globe or a beachball with a line drawn around the center to represent the equator. Darken the room and place a lamp on a table. Remove any shades on the windows.

Explain that our planet is tilted slightly. Tilt the ball to face the lamp and let students know that this is the angle of the Earth during summer in the Northern hemisphere. Move around the light holding the globe or ball at the same angle, stopping at each quarter distance to show fall, winter, and spring. Lead your students in a discussion about whether there would be seasons if the Earth were not tilted.

STAR PATTERNS

Class Experiment .....

Students can even see constellations in the daytime with this activity.

Materials: an empty cereal box; a pencil; a flashlight

What to Do: Copy the Cassiopeia constellation (shown at left) onto the bottom of the cereal box by drawing dots for the stars. Use the pencil to punch holes in the dots. In a darkened room, hold the flashlight and slip it into the top of the box so light shines through the holes at the bottom. Turn the light toward the wall, and you should see the constellation there.

Tell your students that one Greek myth tells the story of a queen named Cassiopeia, who often bragged about how beautiful she was. Cassiopeia was often seen sitting on a throne looking into a mirror. Cassiopeia can be seen sitting on her throne part of the year. But most of the year, she appears upside down as a punishment for her bragging. During the fall, it is easy to recognize Cassiopeia because she forms an easy-to-recognize *W* in the sky.

DISCOVERY: THE NORTH STAR

Class Activity

Students can make a star map that will aid them in finding the North Star (or other constellations or individual stars in the night sky).

Materials: a copy of page 69 for each student or group; dark, heavy construction paper; a pencil; a white crayon; a flashlight; red cellophane; a rubber band

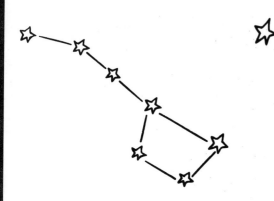

What to Do: Have students copy the Big Dipper onto the construction paper with the crayon. Then let them punch holes in all of the spots where stars appear. On a clear, moonless night, students can take their star chart and a flashlight outdoors. They'll cover the front of the flashlight with red cellophane held in place with a rubber band and shine the light behind the paper so that the holes appear as points of light. They can look for a pattern of stars that matches the chart. Once they have discovered the Big Dipper, they will see two stars at the front of the "bowl." They point directly to the North Star.

BULLETIN BOARD IDEA—THE SUN

Class Activity

Ask students if they know which star is closest to Earth. Explain that the sun is our nearest star and we depend on it for many things. Have a student draw a large picture of the sun or cut one from construction paper. Pin it to the center of the bulletin board. Ask students to bring in magazine pictures or drawings that show ways that the sun is important. (**Example:** for heat, light, solar energy, and for its part in **photosynthesis**) Also post a list of solar facts. (See those listed at the right.)

- average distance from Earth—93 million miles
- diameter at poles—864,000 miles
- age—4.5 billion years
- rotation at equator—25 days
- surface temperature—10,000 degrees Fahrenheit

EATING LIGHT

Class Experiment

One way to demonstrate how important the sun is to life on Earth is to show its value to plants.

Materials: one potted plant; two 1-inch cardboard circles; clay; a sunny window

What to Do: Using clay, stick the cardboard circles onto two different leaves of the plant. Place the plant in a sunny window and care for it normally. After a few days, remove the cardboard circles.

Results: The leaves under the circles will be yellowed from lack of sunlight. Remind students that plants need sunlight to make food, and that either directly or indirectly, most animal life depends on plants for survival.

Discovery: The North Star

For centuries, people have enjoyed spending time gazing into the night sky. It is fun to learn the star groups and patterns to be found there. One very important star to learn is the North Star. Sailors have often used it to help them find their way at night without a compass. The North Star isn't easy to find unless you know where to look. Here's how to use a **very famous star group** called the Big Dipper to point the way.

Materials:

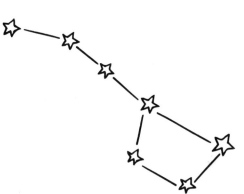

a piece of dark, heavy construction paper
a white crayon
a pencil
a flashlight
a six-inch square piece of red cellophane
a rubber band

What to Do:

1. Copy the pattern of the Big Dipper onto the construction paper using the crayon.

2. With the pencil, punch holes in all the stars.

3. Cover the front of the flashlight with red cellophane held in place with a rubber band.

Now you are ready to find the North Star. The best time to look is on a clear night with no moon. Stand facing the spot where the sun set, then turn toward your right shoulder. That is north. Shine the light behind the paper so that the holes appear as points of light. Look for a pattern of stars that matches the chart. Once you have discovered the Big Dipper, you will see two stars at the front of the "bowl." They point directly to the North Star.

Something to Know:

When you are outside at night, it takes about 30 minutes for your eyes to get used to the dark so that you can see well. If you turn on a flashlight in that time, you have to start over again. Red light won't bother your eyes as much, so covering a flashlight with red cellophane helps you keep your night vision!

SOLAR ECLIPSE

Use this demonstration to explain to students that a solar eclipse occurs when the moon passes between the sun and the Earth.

Materials: a tennis ball; a coin; a lamp; a darkened room

What to Do: Have students take turns pretending they are the Earth. At a distance of about 10 feet from the lamp, have them hold the tennis ball out at arm's length and move it until it is directly between them and their view of the sun (lamp). If students ask how something as small as the moon can block their view of the sun, explain that it is because the moon is much closer. Have them close one eye and use a coin held at arm's length to block out their view of a distant building.

THE PHASES OF THE MOON

Your students will certainly have noticed that the moon appears to change over the course of a month. This activity will help them discover that the moon is always lit the same amount. It is our view of the lit surface that changes.

Materials: a flashlight; a tennis ball

What to Do: The flashlight is the sun. In a darkened room, prop the flashlight slightly higher than the top of your head. Wedging it between some books on a tall shelf will be fine. Stand with your back to the flashlight. You are the Earth. Hold the tennis ball (the moon) at arm's length and about shoulder height in front of you. This is an example of the full moon. If you turn to one side, you will see a half-moon phase. When you face the flashlight, the side of the ball which you can see is completely dark. That is how the moon looks during the phase of the new moon.

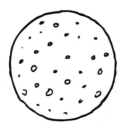 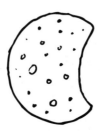 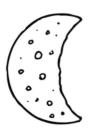  

DISCOVERY: MOONLIGHT

Help students understand that the moon does not shine with a light of its own with this activity.

Materials: a copy of page 71 for each student or group; a flashlight; clay; a hand mirror; a table in a corner

What to Do: Darken the room if possible. Place the hand mirror in the clay so that it stands up and faces outward. Stand at a slight angle to the mirror and turn on the flashlight. Direct the beam at the mirror.

Results: A circle of light will appear on the wall next to the table. The light is from the flashlight, reflected from the surface of the mirror.

Discovery: Moonlight

Stars such as our sun are luminous (LOO-min-us). They give off their own light. Our moon does not give off its own light. The moonlight we see is reflected sunlight.

Materials:

a flashlight
a hand mirror
modeling clay
a table in a corner

What to Do:

1. Darken the room if you can.

2. Put a ball of clay on the table and stand the mirror upright in the clay so that the mirror faces outward.

3. Stand at a slight angle to the mirror and turn on the flashlight.

4. Direct the beam at the mirror. Turn the light on and then off.

5. Note that for a moment, there is a circle of light on the wall.

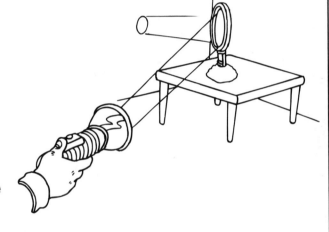

Does the mirror produce its own light? _____

_____

Where is the light coming from? _____

_____

If the moon does not produce its own light, where does the light come from?

_____

_____

SCALE MODEL

You can make a scale model of the Earth and the moon. From a piece of heavy cardboard, cut two circles (one 2 inches in diameter, one 1/2 inch in diameter). Now cut a piece of string 59 inches long and tape each end to one of the circles. Tape the Earth (2-inch circle) to the wall. Tape the string in several places as you move around the room until the moon (1/2-inch circle) is also in place. This model will give your class an idea of the difference in size and the distance between the Earth and its satellite.

MEASURING THE MOON

Sometimes the moon looks larger on the horizon. Is it really larger? Here's a way to measure. Have your students do this nighttime activity as a homework assignment.

Materials: a flat piece of glass from a picture frame with the edges taped for safety; a crayon or marker

What to Do: As the moon appears over the horizon, hold the glass out at arm's length and trace its shape on the glass with the marker. After the moon is high in the sky, look at it again through the glass. It will fit perfectly into the circle you drew earlier.

MATH LINK

The pull of the moon's gravity is one-sixth that of Earth's. If you weigh 60 pounds on Earth, you would weigh 10 pounds on the moon. Have students figure out how much they would weigh on the moon.

SPOTLIGHT ON SCIENTISTS

Give your students copies of page 73 and have them read the story about Benjamin Banneker. Explain that at the time he lived, African-Americans were rarely given the opportunity to get an education. Even so, Banneker made a tremendous contribution to the study of stars and weather. As a homework assignment, ask students to find information about another important African-American scientist.

THE PLANETS

Remembering the sentence below will help students recall the names and order of the planets (Mercury, Venus, Earth, Mars, Jupiter, Saturn, Uranus, Neptune, Pluto). Tell them to picture the scene in their minds.

My **V**ery **E**ducated **M**other **J**ust **S**erved **U**s **N**ine **P**izzas.

TEAMWORK

Divide your class into nine teams. Assign each team a planet (including Earth). Have each team work together to find information on the planet and give a report to the class.

FS-23213 Science Made Simple ▪ © Frank Schaffer Publications, Inc.

Spotlight On Scientists

Benjamin Banneker was born November 9, 1731, in Maryland. Even as a child, he was good with numbers. As he grew older, he became fascinated with astronomy and taught himself to use some simple instruments. He would study in the daytime and stargaze at night. In 1792, he published the first edition of Benjamin Banneker's Almanack. An almanac is a book with valuable information about weather conditions, phases of the Moon, eclipses, and tides, as well as stories, puzzles, riddles, and more.

The almanac was a great accomplishment for Banneker, but he took a break from it for a few months. During that time, he used his mathematical skills to help plan the city of Washington, D.C. From then on, he became a friend to Thomas Jefferson, and they exchanged letters often on scientific matters. Benjamin Banneker published the last issue of his famous almanac in 1802.

Benjamin Banneker's almanac was filled with information and stories about the stars and weather. Imagine that you are going to make your own almanac. Using the knowledge you have gained about the Earth and the solar system, provide information that would help a farmer or a sailor do his or her job.

_____

_____

_____

_____

_____

_____

_____

_____

_____

A MODEL SOLAR SYSTEM

Using cardboard and clay, you can make a small scale model of the solar system. Cut a sun about five feet in diameter out of butcher paper. Make the planets from clay according to the chart below. Explain that even at this size, the relative distances between the planets and the sun are too great to fit in the classroom. Pluto would have to be a distance equal to more than three football fields away.

Mercury	1/8 inch
Venus	5/16 inch
Earth	5/16 inch
Mars	3/16 inch
Jupiter	3 3/8 inches
Saturn	2 3/4 inches (without rings)
Uranus	1 1/8 inches
Neptune	1 1/8 inches
Pluto	1/8 inch

ORBITS

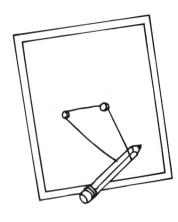

A planet's orbit is the curved path it follows around the sun. Point out to students that the orbits of the planets are not circles but ellipses. Use this activity to demonstrate how to draw an ellipse.

Materials: two tacks; a 10-inch-long piece of string; a piece of cardboard at least 8 ½" x 11"; plain paper; a pencil

What to Do: Place a piece of paper on the cardboard, then push the two tacks in the center about two inches apart. Tie a knot in the string to form a loop and place it around the tacks. Put the pencil just inside the loop and pull the string out as far as it will go. Try to draw a circle. You will actually draw an ellipse.

MERCURY'S CRATERS

The surface of Mercury is pitted with many crater impacts. Because it has virtually no atmosphere, nothing wears the craters away. This demonstration will show how craters form.

Materials: a large bowl; flour; newspapers; marbles or small stones of different sizes; a tennis ball

What to Do: Spread newspapers on the floor to catch any mess. Put about two cups of flour in the bowl and place it on the newspapers. Have a student stand over the bowl and drop stones, marbles, and finally the tennis ball into the flour to see what sort of craters form. Explain that the objects represent meteoroids and other space rocks that have battered the tiny planet since it formed.

FS-23213 Science Made Simple ▪ © Frank Schaffer Publications, Inc.

DISCOVERY: THE RED PLANET

Mars is known as the red planet because of the reddish color of its soil. The color is the result of the oxidation of iron. Have students use page 76 to see the process in action.

Materials: a copy of page 76 for each student; a steel wool scouring pad with the soap rinsed out; a paper towel; a small glass bowl; water; a rubber glove

What to Do: Place the paper towel in the bowl. Soak the pad, then leave it in the bowl for several days. Once it has begun to rust, let it dry. Wearing a glove, rub the pad between your fingers to show the red dust.

MARS-SCAPE

Class Activity

It's easy to design your own class "Mars-scape." First, fill the top of a shoebox with sand and scatter small rocks and pebbles on top. Next, you need one or two soft steel wool scouring pads with the soap rinsed out. Cut the pad into very small bits and mix them in with the sand. With a spray bottle, moisten the surface with water and keep it damp for several days. The metal from the scouring pad will soon form rust and your landscape will take on a reddish hue.

BULLETIN BOARD IDEA

Group Activity

Convert the bulletin board into a large chart with six columns labeled across the top: *Diameter; Period of Rotation; Length of Year; Distance From the Sun; Number of Moons; Fun Fact.* List the names of the planets down the left side. Divide the class into nine groups. Have each group fill in the information for one planet.

THE RED SPOT

Class Experiment

One of Jupiter's most famous features is its Big Red Spot, a storm in the planet's atmosphere. It is most likely something like a super hurricane. This demonstration shows how it moves in Jupiter's atmosphere.

Materials: a large glass jar; water; a pencil; red glitter

What to Do: Fill the jar with water. Pour in about two tablespoons of glitter. Use the pencil to rapidly stir the water in small circles.

Results: The glitter will start to swirl into a funnel shape. By stirring, you are creating a vortex (a whirling mass) that draws the glitter toward the center.

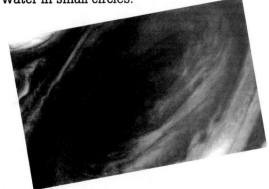

Discovery: The Red Planet

Mars is known as the red planet. Have you ever seen rust? Rust forms when iron combines with oxygen, a gas. Iron in Martian soil has combined with oxygen to make a rust-colored dust. Winds lift the red dust into the Martian atmosphere, often giving it a pinkish color. Here's how to see this process for yourself.

Materials:
   a steel wool scouring pad with the soap rinsed out
   a paper towel
   a small glass bowl
   water
   a rubber glove

What to Do:
   1. Place the paper towel in the bowl.

   2. Soak the scouring pad and leave it in the bowl for a few days.

   3. Once the pad has begun to rust, let it dry.

   4. Wearing a glove, rub the pad between your fingers to see the red dust.

Describe what you think it might be like to spend a day on Mars.

_____

_____

_____

_____

_____

_____

_____

_____

_____

_____

FS-23213 Science Made Simple • © Frank Schaffer Publications, Inc.

A COMET'S TAIL

Class Experiment

As a comet nears the sun, the gases warm and begin to glow, and a long tail may form. The tail is "blown" by the solar wind and streams out behind the comet as it approaches the sun and in front of it as it moves away. To demonstrate this, you will need a fan with a protective grating, and a Styrofoam or rubber ball with several long ribbons attached. Turn the fan on at a low speed. Hold the ball and approach the fan. The ribbons will begin to stream out behind the ball. After you circle around the fan and begin to move away, the ribbons will stream out in front of you.

BULLETIN BOARD IDEA

Class Activity

Introduce students to the long history of space travel by creating a time line of the past 40 years across the top of the board. You might begin with the launch of *Sputnik*. As a homework assignment, have students look up and learn a little about one space mission, such as one of the *Mercury* flights, *Apollo 11*, or one of the *Viking* probes. Then have students write their information on 3" x 5" cards. Pin the cards on the board in order of occurrence, and run yarn up to the time line to show in which year the mission took place. Decorate the board with photos of spacecraft and astronauts.

Apollo 11

Apollo 12

Apollo 13

ROCKETS AWAY

Class Activity

Just for fun, have students build their own balloon rockets. Explain that an important law of motion is "For every action, there is an equal and opposite reaction." Ask how that might apply to rocket launches.

Materials: a copy of page 78 for each student or group; an oblong balloon; plastic fishing line; a plastic drinking straw; tape; a paper clip

What to Do: Slip a drinking straw onto the fishing line, then tie off the line so that it stretches unhindered for at least 10 feet. Try to have as little sag as possible in the line. Blow up the balloon and use the paper clip to secure the end. Tape the balloon rocket to the straw on the line. Remove the paper clip and release the rocket.

Rockets Away

Follow these directions to make a rocket that is easy to put together and launch across the room.

Materials:
 an oblong balloon
 plastic fishing line
 a plastic drinking straw
 tape
 a paper clip

What to Do:

1. Slip a drinking straw onto the fishing line, then tie the line to something at each end so that it stretches for at least 10 feet.

2. Blow up the balloon and use the paper clip to close the end.

3. Tape the balloon rocket to the straw on the line.

4. Remove the paper clip and release the rocket.

Humankind has always been curious about the Earth and its neighbor planets. Scientists have built and launched many spacecraft and probes to explore the solar system. Use this space to write about what it might be like to visit your favorite planet.

_____

_____

_____

_____

_____

_____

_____

_____

_____

FS-23213 Science Made Simple ▪ © Frank Schaffer Publications, Inc.